SLAYING THE
LAW SCHOOL
DRAGON

SLAYING THE LAW SCHOOL DRAGON

How to Survive—And Thrive—In First-Year Law School

Second Edition

George Roth

John Wiley & Sons, Inc.
New York • Chichester • Brisbane • Toronto • Singapore

In recognition of the importance of preserving what has
been written, it is a policy of John Wiley & Sons,
Inc. to have books of enduring value published in
the United States printed on acid-free paper, and
we exert our best efforts to that end.

Copyright © 1980, 1991 by George Roth
Published by John Wiley & Sons, Inc.
First published by Dodd, Mead & Company.

This publication is designed to provide accurate and
authoritative information in regard to the subject
matter covered. It is sold with the understanding that
the publisher is not engaged in rendering legal, accounting,
or other professional services. If legal advice or other
expert assistance is required, the services of a competent
professional person should be sought.

*From a Declaration of Principles jointly adopted by a
Committee of the American Bar Association and a
Committee of Publishers.*

Library of Congress Cataloging-in-Publication Data

Roth, George J.
    Slaying the law school dragon : how to survive—and
    thrive—in first-year law school—2nd edition. / by George Roth.
        p.   cm.
    Includes bibliographical references and index.
    ISBN 0 471–54298–9
        1. Law students—United States—Handbooks, manuals,
    etc.   2. Law schools—United States.   3. Law—Study
    and teaching—United States.
    I. Title.
    KF283.R68   1991
    340′.088375—dc20   90–23358
                                                          CIP

Printed in the United States of America.
91 92 10 9 8 7 6 5 4 3 2 1

To GREG and JIM and their families

PREFACE TO THE SECOND EDITION

When I started to write the first edition of this book some twelve years ago, students at most law schools were frequently confronted by uncaring, imperious professors whose sole goal seemed to be to create an aura of constant harassment, presumably based on an old theory that such a setting would better acclimate the students to the rigors of the courtroom. There was little of the one-on-one contact found in other graduate academic disciplines, practically no first year orientation of any kind was available, and there was much not-too-subtle hostility toward women students. An almost warlike "us against them" philosophy prevailed in the lecture halls. In retrospect, it appears that this atmosphere represented the tail end of a dying, century-old legal pedagogy which, interestingly enough, became celebrated in several novels and television productions before its demise.

Today, a more harmonious environment prevails. Most professors seem willing to help and work with students; more and more law schools are running pre–law school summer classes for new enrollees; and sexist traditions are abating. The custom, for example, of embarrassing women students in class by selectively having them give the facts in salacious cases no longer exists.

What remain, however, are the pressures and anxieties created by the tremendous workload, compared to what the student has been accustomed to in college courses; the need to learn an entirely new language, expressed in English but frequently employing novel meanings and concepts; the lack of knowledge of where the student stands academically; the ever-present awareness that anything studied may come up somewhere in a Bar Exam question; and the knowledge that every classmate is a direct competitor for the same few good jobs. These worries are the fire, teeth, and claws of the Law School Dragon. That is where the battle lies.

This new edition, like the first, which has been used by thousands of students before you, can be the sword and shield with which you can slay the Dragon and confidently walk the path to becoming a successful lawyer.

* * *

A big thanks to Betty, Art, Greg, and Jeff Roth, and to Mitchell M. Cnota, librarian of the California Attorney General's Office, for their help in preparing this second edition.

George Roth

CONTENTS

1

WHY YOU NEED THIS BOOK

Annually, thousands of new students enter law schools all over the country. But a tremendous number never pass their first year. Some drop out; others flunk out. The rigorous admission process has ensured that they are almost all good students and probably have higher than average intelligence. Most are extremely motivated. Some have already had successful careers. So why the high disaster rate? What is the trouble? Can anything be done to remedy the situation?

The answer to the last question is a resounding YES! That is what this book is all about. If you follow its advice and adapt its suggestions to your own personality, the chances are good that you will stay in school, pass the bar, and go on to a rewarding professional career.

Whether you have already been accepted into a law school, are awaiting answers to your applications, or are just thinking about applying, this book is for you.

Hovering over all law schools, lurking in lecture hall corners, and sometimes even invading the minds and bodies of law school students is the ominous and vicious Law School Dragon. The dragon has many arms: fear, anxiety, inordinate competition, lack of time, memory lapse, to cite just a few examples.

There is the fear of failure, of being unable to adapt to the rigors of law school, of not getting good grades; there is anxiety caused by intense pressure to keep up with the daily work; the inordinate competition with ones' classmates (the best students get the best job offers); the lack of time to do all the daily case briefing, outside assignments, and extracurricular work that make for a full and rewarding academic experience; the inability to remember all the facts and rules of the cases and the various distinctions and applications of legal principles.

In this book I show you how to slay your personal Law School Dragon. Once you kill it you will be better able to appreciate how insidiously it attacks your fellow students and makes some of them fall off the path to success.

I present an overview of how law school works. I tell you what happens in class; describe the various types of law books; give you pointers on how to study so you better understand what you read and what the professors are talking about. I explain how to organize and remember your work and give tips on how to handle exams; and I help you build the self-confidence that you will need to succeed in school and, eventually, in practice.

This book illustrates a novel method of study, readily adaptable to your own inclinations, that will enable you to do your case assignments with a minimum of writing, so that the knowledge stays in your head instead of in your notebook. The method facilitates a clear understanding of why each case is in your casebook, why it is important in the development of that particular legal subject, and what it portends for the future development of the law. I have included two actual cases in the text to give you a clear idea of the type of material you will be exposed to in your daily reading assignments, and to allow you to practice the study method I suggest.

You will get a capsulized view of the four major first-year courses: contracts, torts, crimes and property, along with a brief introduction to constitutional law. You will learn how almost every course has its roots in the *common law* of England, and you will see actual examples of old English *writs* and *pleadings* which will make it easier for you to comprehend what law professors frequently refer to, but rarely illustrate, in class. You will learn that the *cases* you will be reading are the *opinions* of appellate court justices. You will see how these opinions are developed from the written arguments of lawyers for each side, called *briefs*. You will see how briefs are composed. You will learn how you can compose winning briefs for your own Moot Court work in law school.

To help you plan your career, there are chapters that describe various types of law practice, show how to pick a place to practice, and suggest ways to get clients.

If you adapt the advice and suggestions in the following pages to your own style and personality, the odds are high that you will be among those academically gowned seniors singing the alma mater on graduation day, and that you will pass the bar and will join the great fellowship of lawyers who have preceded you in your endeavors.

You may be interested in why some people fail to graduate. Among the unfortunates are those who are not temperamentally compatible with the demands of law school: those who lack the ability to think flexibly within a rigidly structured framework; those who cannot adapt emotionally to the necessity of trying to make logic out of what may appear to them to be an inequitable result; those who will not relax and accept the law school method for what it is; those who cannot occasionally sit back and laugh at the whole thing. Some students may have to take outside employment in order to get the money for tuition, books and living expenses, and find the time constraints too great to manage. Others may be unable to keep the delicate balance between attention to a spouse and children on one hand, and the depth of concentration required just to get through law school on the other. The old adage "The law is a jealous mistress" applies to more than families, however; it covers all outside interests.

So much for the negatives. What about the positives? They are there, they are great, and they are fascinating. The study of law gives you a look into every phase of human experience. You will become familiar with the methods that Western civilization has developed and used to make agreements, settle disputes, protect individual rights, govern conduct, protect property, transfer land and personalty, compensate individuals for harm done to them by others, and enable business and governmental organizations to operate. You will gain a profound respect for words: their meanings, nuances, and usages. You will learn to think like a lawyer. Most important, however, is that you will realize you will be in a wonderful position to contribute something constructive to society.

Are you ready for the task? Buckle on your mental armor, and with this book as your shield, join me now in slaying the Law School Dragon.

2

WHAT TO DO BEFORE SCHOOL STARTS

Get started as early as possible. Four weeks is not too much time to give yourself, as there is a lot to do. In this and the next few chapters, I give you some suggestions to help you spend this time profitably.

If you are not going to be living in a dorm, get yourself the best accommodations you can afford. It may be unrealistic to expect anyone to move in a month in advance, but it would be prudent to make your arrangements as early as possible before the crowd gets there. Try to get a room close to the university law library. That is where you will be spending your after-class hours, and the less time you waste trudging back and forth, the more you will have for work and study.

Look for a place that is relatively quiet. You will need as much sleep as you can get, and when you are studying in your room you will need an atmosphere that lets you concentrate on difficult work. I had a small apartment at the start of my second year of law school that looked pretty good when I took it. After a music major moved in next door, along with his African drums, Chinese oboe, several other instruments, loud stereos, and lots of wine-bearing visitors, it

5

became a great place for fun, but not exactly the ideal spot to concentrate on the learned writings of Supreme Court justices. Soon I was spending more time at my neighbor's place than my own. If I had not moved to new quarters I am sure I would have flunked out that semester.

Besides your apartment, check out all the cheap restaurants, pizza places, beer joints, water holes, and singles bars in the neighborhood. Find one or two really good places to dine out. Do these things now, as you will not have much time later. Do not forget the markets, drugstores, movies, gyms, emergency medical set-up, and anything else you might need. You can do most of this at night and on weekends.

As soon as possible, get a list of the casebooks that you will be using and then go out and buy them. Make sure you get the right edition. Off-campus prices may be cheaper; but be careful, especially of sidewalk vendors, who are notorious for passing off stale material.

Sometime before the first day of class you should devote time to checking out things around school itself, and also to visiting the local county courthouse and the state appellate court, if there is one nearby.

On campus, see if any professors are around, particularly those you may have this semester; introduce yourself and try to get acquainted. Say hello to the administrators and clerical help in the office. Ask everyone you meet for any tips that might help you get through the first year. Occasionally you will pick up some valuable information. If you have the time and inclination, go into the empty lecture hall where your class will be held. You might want to sit in a few different seats to find your preference and then, if you feel it is important enough, get there early on the first day of class and claim it.

Spend a few hours looking around the law library. Get to know the librarians. Most are pretty helpful. Browse around the different parts of the stacks and thumb through the various types of law books. (These are discussed at some length in the next chapter.) Find out where the best carrells are for you to work. Look out for drafty air conditioning outlets, areas where there will be too much visual stimulation, noise, student traffic, and other distractions. This personal environmental impact survey could be extremely worthwhile. Think of yourself as an embryo and the library as your womb-home for the next three years.

When you visit the county courthouse, ask the clerk to show you how the *litigation indices* work. Take a look at a few civil and criminal files. One thing that may come as a surprise is that a lawsuit ultimately boils down to a bunch of papers. An appellate court looked at a similar bunch of papers to reach the decision printed in your casebook. On this early visit do not make any attempt to understand the material in the files. But do notice the titles: Complaint, Temporary Restraining Order, Demurrer, Answer, Motion, and so on. You will see that everything is presented formally. Be aware that some underlying controversy is the reason why each case is before the court.

All of this will give you a better grasp of what you will be studying later on. You may note that some lawyers seem to have put more work into their cases than others. While it is not always true, it usually works out that the most thoroughly prepared are the ones who win.

When you are through looking at the files, go upstairs to the county law library. Get acquainted with the librarian, who could be of great help to you during your entire law school career. For example, if a professor assigns outside reading and there is a big waiting list at the school library, a friendly county law librarian may lend you a copy from the court library, or perhaps even get you one through the state library book exchange. This librarian could save you the outdated *advance sheets*—the paperback copies of the current appellate court opinions, which come out before the bound volumes—which would give you a little home library of the latest cases to supplement those printed in your casebooks.

If some other enterprising individual is already receiving the advance sheets, try stopping in at a few of the law firms in town to see if they will give you their throwaways. It is another source to tap and could give you a future job contact.

The state appellate court may not be close enough to the law school to visit, and if you do get to it, it may not be in session.

However, if it is accessible, go. You will at least be able to check out the files. You will note that each of these appellate cases contains a copy of the trial court clerk's record, a stenographic transcript of the trial court testimony and the briefs filed by each side. A completed case also will contain a copy of the appellate court's opinion.

County trial courts rarely write opinions, and those they do write are not accorded much respect as legal authority. In the federal system, however, District Court judges often write opinions. Their views are accorded intellectual value and are often used to bolster legal reasoning and arguments expounded by state and federal appellate courts. The casebooks you will use contain selected opinions of the appellate courts. Appellate opinions have precedential value in the jurisdictions where they are issued. They are also persuasive to decision writers in other geographic areas of the country. As of the date they are written, they contain the latest judicial thinking on the legal issues involved.

3

BROWSING AROUND
THE LAW BOOKS

Collected *reports* of *cases* are periodically published under the direct authority of the courts that issue them. They are known as the "official" reports. Copies of official reports are also commercially published and distributed. The West Publishing Company issues reports for blocks of states: Atlantic, Southern, Pacific, and so on. Through a system of cross-pagination one can quickly refer to the actual volume and page of the official reports.

Besides appearing in book form, the reports are also available through computer services. By punching a few keys, a busy lawyer can quickly pull a case; directly incorporate some of the text into a document then in preparation; have a personal law library available whenever needed; and eliminate expensive shelving and storage space. Two major computer systems are now offered to the profession, *WESTLAW* and *LEXIS*. Each contains the cases from the reports verbatim; however, for competitive reasons, each claims to have unique features that make it more facile than the other. But even though the opinions are now available through computers, they appear as pages in law books. It is still necessary to know how to look up cases the old-fashioned way.

Every case in the reports has a title which shows the name of the parties, which court issued the opinion, the year of issuance, and where the case can be found. This information is translated into cryptographic numbers and letters called a *citation*.

Here's how it works: In 1924, the Minnesota Supreme Court decided the case of *Hanson* v. *Johnson*. Its opinion is reported in Volume 161 of the official Minnesota State Supreme Court Reports beginning at page 229. It is also reported in Volume 201 of West's Northwestern Reports at page 322. The full, formal citation is *Hanson* v. *Johnson*, 161 Minn. 229, 201 N.W.322 (1924).

Often you will see a citation like 14 Cal 3d 62, or 38 F2d 641. The 3d means that in California there are three series of state supreme court reports, each of the first two series having a large number of volumes. Similarly, F2d refers to Federal Reporter, Second Series.

There is a unique citation for every case, and if a case is reported somewhere, it is possible to locate it. Law schools have reports for the entire United States. Most also have the old English cases, which are still valuable for tracing the historical development of legal principles. The bigger the library, the more it has available. Through the library exchange system it is possible to get a copy of almost any case that is reported.

In your study of cases, you may come across a situation where the particular *jurisdiction* in which the case arose has a practice of reversing the names of the parties on appeal. If you are not aware of this possibility, you may be confused when you try to put the facts together with the *holding*. In the *trial court*, the name of the plaintiff (the person who started the suit) appears first. In some appellate courts, the same case name is retained: in others, the appellant's name is first. The latter situation existed in the *Hanson* case, cited above. Fortunately, the text of the opinion made it easy to determine who was the plaintiff.

Something else that may cause confusion is the New York practice of referring to the county level trial court as the Supreme Court and its judges as "justices." The highest court in New York is known as the Court of Appeals. It is staffed by justices. In most other states the highest court is called the Supreme Court and is also staffed by justices.

In the old English reports, the name of the set of reports is usually taken from the name of the person who edited the series. Sometimes it is taken from the name of the court. Many of the cases show the plaintiff as *Rex* v. ---, or *Regina* v. ---. This does not mean that Rex and Regina were unusually litigious persons. "Rex" means "King"; "Regina" means "Queen". In the United States, the title *State* v. --- or *People* v. --- is used when the state government brings a law suit, and *United States* v. --- when the federal government does.

By the way, here is a bit of one-upmanship to put into your portfolio. From 1790 through 1874, the first 90 volumes of the collected opinions of the United States Supreme Court were not numbered consecutively. Instead, like the old English reports, they were named after the reporter of decisions who issued them and given small clusters of numbers as they were published. Thus, between 1790 and 1800 four volumes appeared under the name of Dallas, and we get a citation like 2 Dall. ____, for example. The other reporters were Cranch, 1801–1815, nine (5–13 U.S.); Wheaton, 1816–1827, twelve (14–25 U.S.); Peters, 1828–1842, sixteen (26–41 U.S.); Howard, 1843–1860, twenty–four (42–65 U.S.); Black, 1861–1862, two (66–67 U.S.); Wallace, 1863–1874 twenty-three (68–90 U.S.). Beginning in 1875 the name of the reports was changed to United States Supreme Court Reports. The first 90 volumes were issued as an appendix and numbering started with volume 91. Over the years, there have been some reprints (and rebindings) where the first 90 volumes were numbered consecutively, as indicated above. This information, for you serious readers, does not need to be memorized. I have just put it in here so you can have some fun if you want to, and when one of your classmates makes a reference to a case in 46 U.S. you can say in a very sophisticated, knowledgeable way, "Oh, yes. Howard was the reporter then, wasn't he?"

This one-upmanship business is not as frivolous as it might seem. Because most schools give no quizzes or exams until the final (though some professors may give an occasional mid-term), few students have any idea where they stand compared to their class-mates. Thus, there is a tendency to worry a bit. Anything you can do to bolster your own morale, without being obnoxious, will make you that much more relaxed as you go through the semester.

You should, early on, become aware of a book on how to do legal research: how to find out what the law is in some particular area. It will contain a good discussion of the various reports and statutes, sample pages that illustrate the materials referred to in the text, and detailed descriptions of all the methods used to look up the law. You will probably find it in the reference section of the law library. Should you decide to buy one from the several available, check to be sure that, if your school gives a legal research course, it is the book that will be used in that class. But scan some of the others anyway. You may find one that is easier for you to follow.

Along with the reports, you will be exposed to a number of different types of law books. You should become familiar with them as early as possible in your studies.

When the reporter of decisions edits a volume of the reports for publication, the legal points involved are summarized at the beginning of each case in short sentences called *headnotes*. Each headnote is given a consecutive number, which is then inserted into the running text so a reader can quickly turn to that part of the case which may be of special interest. Here are examples of typical headnotes:

The Constitution of the United States is a solemn compact between the States, to be enforced by State legislation, or by judicial action; and State officers whose duty it is to adjudicate or execute the laws are governed by it; and being a part of the supreme law of the land, it is a part of the law of each State.

A wife may impress a homestead on premises held in joint tenancy by herself and her husband, as well as upon his separate property; and once the wife impresses premises with a valid homestead, the husband is without power to destroy it except in the manner provided by statute.

Digests contain headnotes arranged by subject. Each headnote has the citation to the case it came from. Within the legal subtopic under which the case appears, the headnote frequently contains some factual information to illustrate the context that engendered this particular bit of law.

West Publishing Company writes its own headnotes. Each of

these, besides being numbered to a specific part of the text, also has a special number called a Key Number. Each Key Number refers to a particular subsection of some branch of the law. All headnotes having the same Key Number are grouped together, so it is possible to quickly find similar cases from the same jurisdiction, or any broader area which is covered by the digest. Since all West publications use the same system, you can use the Key Number to find what other jurisdictions have done with the same problem. At the back of the digest, there is a table of all cases referred to in the compiled headnotes. Also, this table will direct you to the places in the digest where these cases can be found.

When you are using a digest, remember that it contains only the cases for the period of time and the jurisdiction or geographic area that it covers. In other words, if you are in the New York Digest, you will not find any Ohio case listed or described.

If you have a citation for an American case, there is a valuable series known as *Shepard's Citations* which you can use to find cases in point. These books contain tables of numbers. Get the volume of *Shepard's* for the state or area you are interested in, turn to the volume number of the report in which your case appears, then run down the column until you reach the proper page reference. There you will find a citation to every place where your case is mentioned. Different symbols are printed next to each of the new citations telling whether points in the original case were overruled, agreed with, distinguished, or modified.

Textbooks give an analysis of the law in one subject, such as contracts, torts, corporations, or criminal procedure. Some are in one volume, others are in sets. Frequently the same author writes a one-volume textbook to complement the casebook you are using in class. Generally, each case mentioned in the textbook is summarized in a sentence which gives the pertinent holding in the case. The citation is given in a footnote.

There is a useful series of textbooks known as "hornbooks" which have lead paragraphs or sentences in boldface type emphasizing some principle of law, followed by a discussion citing the relevant cases in point.

Legal encyclopedias are multi-volume sets containing discussions of practically every phase of every law subject. Some cover all states, others only one.

In the old days all law books were published with tan leather bindings. Today, they come in all colors. One of the legends floating around concerns a highly respected lawyer who worked for a firm for fifty years. Every day he would arrive, unlock his desk, look carefully at a little piece of paper, mutter to himself, and then carefully lock the drawer again before commencing his work. One day he died. All the young lawyers rushed over to his desk, broke the lock, and read the piece of paper to find the secret of success the old man had kept hidden for so many years. It said: "West is blue, Deerings is red."

Along with the general group of textbooks is a series called *Restatements of the Law*. These are written by a national assembly of law professors, who watch changes occurring in existing legal principles and then write a suggested interpretation which they hope will be adopted across the country. One of the best things about the *Restatements* for law students is that they contain a number of factual situations written in simple language to illustrate the point the authors wish to make. A word of caution, however: do not read the technical explanations too early into your schooling. You will find them totally confusing because of your limited experience. Just look at the boldface type and the short examples.

The law is divided generally into two parts: constitutions, *statutes, ordinances,* regulations, on the one hand; and what the judges say these mean—their interpretations—on the other. Judge-made law, found in the opinions in the reports, is sometimes referred to as "modern common law."

The laws and ordinances enacted by Congress, state legislatures, county boards of supervisors, city councils, district commissions, and so on, along with the administrative regulations of operating departments of these branches of government, are set forth in books known as statutes, *codes,* ordinances and regulations. Annotated volumes have citations to pertinent cases.

Law reviews are periodicals put out by the different law schools. They usually contain one or more long articles by experienced lawyers and professors on various legal subjects, along with notes written by students covering recent developments in the law. The students with top grades act as an editorial board and, under faculty guidance, publish the law review. If you are asked to write for the law review, do it. The experience is terrific and the prestige may help you get a good job after graduation. Law review articles contain excellent background information about areas of the law you may be concerned with and will also give you ideas on new trends and concepts. Ideas in law review articles are often adopted later as the basis of court decisions.

Law review articles and notes are thoroughly researched and give a fairly good list of important cases related to the main issues discussed. Generally, there is a citation to every statement made. Whenever you have a spare moment, read those articles that apply to the courses you are working on. The best way to find law review material which relates to a subject in which you are interested is to look it up in the Index to Legal Periodicals or one of the several computer services.

In the back of this book I have listed a broad spectrum of well-developed and highly informative law review articles, arranged according to areas you will be studying. Do not ignore them. Even though some were published years ago, they can clear up a lot of problems you may run into trying to understand sometimes esoteric and mysterious subjects.

You may have occasion, while going through some form of internship, to draw up pleading and practice documents or various types of legal agreements. There are various collections of form books available for models. While you are browsing through your school library, thumb through a few of these volumes so you know what is available. Always remember, if you do use them, that they are only samples. Do not get trapped into following them slavishly, word for word.

For recreational reading, you might enjoy the *Mr. Tutt* stories by Arthur Train. He takes a legal point and wraps an excellent tale around it. It is all common law–related, so you learn some background. Train wrote primarily in the 1920s. You can probably get these books at the regular library.

When I was a student, I came across a dusty old package in the

15

attic of my home county library bearing the seal of the county clerk impregnated in red wax. It contained a set of books written around 1900. Pasted on the outside of the package was a news clipping, musty with age, which told that the Board of Supervisors had ordered the librarian to keep this set out of circulation permanently because the author had taken important criminal cases and fictionalized them to show how criminals could beat the law. I got the librarian's permission to open the package and found that they were great stories which gave me a good insight into the common law background of the criminal procedure course. The leading character, Randolph Mason, would advise his clients exactly what to do when committing crimes, so that because of some legal technicality they could not later be convicted. Each story was cited to an actual case. I guess the Board of Supervisors believed that you should not teach a robber how to steal, at least not through the county library.

Always be on the lookout for this type of material. It makes for relaxing and enjoyable reading and you may learn something while you read. In fact, spending some spare time occasionally, reading anything that happens to be available at the moment, may sometimes prove profitable in the future. After all, law as a profession encompasses all human activity—you never know when something you read will be the subject of a case—and the broader your base, the more apt you will be to come up with an understandable solution to whatever problem presents itself for analysis.

I once used an article on time travel from the Mathematical Games section of *Scientific American*. At issue was whether a contractor, whose license had expired because of nonpayment of the annual fee, could still qualify as low bidder on a state construction job if he reactivated his license retroactively. The state's position was that the State Contract Act required all bidders to be licensed at the time of bid, and therefore, it would be improper to consider him a duly qualified bidder, because his status was not equal to that of the other bidders at the time the actual bid was made. The low bidder argued that the Contractors License Act permitted retroactive reinstatement for all purposes upon payment of the late annual license fee. Obviously, there was an inherent conflict in the two statutes which the Legislature had not foreseen.

The magazine article I used pointed out that, if you went back in time and just were an observer, there would be no problem when you returned to the present. But if you went back in time and changed material facts (killed your grandfather, perhaps), you never could reexist in the present because you never would have been born. This paradox has been solved by science fiction writers through the use of the literary device of describing two phases of existence—changing prior facts splits everything thereafter into two parallel worlds, one real and one imaginary. I successfully argued that retroactive reinstatement of the contractor, to give him a valid license at the time of the bid opening (when in reality he did not have one), was the same kind of paradoxical time travel; acceptance of his theory of the law would put him into the world of fantasy.

4

WHERE THE CASES COME FROM

Before we go any further, you should know something about the way law is taught in American law schools.

The basis of the American law school system is what is known as the case method. In the case method selected published decisions of appellate courts, taken from actual cases, are grouped together by legal subject matter in books known as *casebooks*. The objective of the editors is to choose interesting and informative cases that can be read progressively, to enable the student to observe the historical development of the topic, become aware of the legal reasoning involved, and get familiar with the language used by lawyers and judges in that area of the law. This background of knowledge should give the student a command of what the law is and an ability to predict where it may be headed.

How do these cases we are talking about get into the law books? They start when two people get into an argument that they cannot settle. Eventually, one sues the other and the case comes to trial. A judge or a jury gives a verdict for one side and the losing party appeals to a higher court.

State cases normally begin at county court level; if appealed, they progress to intermediate and supreme state appellate courts; and if a federal or United States constitutional question is involved, they may even get as far as the United States Supreme Court. In the federal system, cases generally start in the United States District Court and are appealed to the Circuit Court of Appeals, and then to the United States Supreme Court. Appellate courts are historically made up of an odd number of justices, generally three, five or seven, depending on the court, with nine sitting on the United States Supreme Court.

When a Notice of Appeal is filed in the trial court, a copy of the trial court record is prepared and filed with the appellate court. The appellant files an opening brief; respondent files an answering brief, and appellant files a reply brief. After the court has had time to study the record and the briefs, the matter is *calendared* (set for oral argument). One lawyer for each side is given equal time to present the case, generally a half hour. No witnesses are presented. Consideration of evidence is limited to what is in the record on appeal.

As each lawyer argues, the justices may, and frequently do, interrupt to ask questions. When time for both sides has expired, the case is "submitted." Eventually, the court issues a written opinion giving its decision in the case. If all the justices agree, the decision is, of course, "unanimous." If there is disagreement, the majority rules in a "split decision." Whatever the result, the case is eventually transferred back down to the trial court for disposition in accordance with the directions of the opinion.

An *opinion* contains holdings on various points of law involved in the case and discusses the legal reasoning involved in reaching the decision. If the appellant wins it means that the trial court erred in the way it handled the case and its decision is *overruled*. If the respondent wins it means that the trial court verdict is affirmed (stands as it originally was rendered). While to the clients and their lawyers the case is a matter of victory or defeat, to other lawyers, the appellate opinion is a guide as to what the latest law is with respect to the subjects discussed.

So that the profession will quickly be aware of any changes in the law, opinions are first published in paperback advance sheets available for purchase. Individual copies of issued opinions may be obtained earlier from the issuing court, and important cases are usually printed the next publication day in legal newspapers within the jurisdiction of the court. In some states like California, where there is sufficient demand for the service, a chain of legal newspapers daily puts out copies of all appellate decisions, just as they appear typed in the court files. When enough material has accumulated, the cases are published in bound volumes. Eventually, selected opinions wind up in student casebooks.

5

HOW TO PREPARE
FOR THE SEMESTER

You should set aside as much time as possible before school starts to prepare for your classes. Used properly, this period could be one of the most productive of the entire semester. You will be able to come to the first lecture with a good lead on most of your fellow students and you will have time available right from the beginning to handle not only the mandatory outside reading assignments, but also the discretionary reference suggestions and extracurricular work which are essential if you want to make better-than-average progress and grades.

Time is the most valuable asset you have as a law student; a relaxed attitude probably comes next. On the other end of the scale, over-anxiety and procrastination can lead to academic bankruptcy. Ideally, you should come to each lecture confident that you are fully prepared on the required work and ready to participate in an intelligent discussion of the subject at hand. You can get close to achieving this goal by using your own adaptation of a method I developed as a student and which I have refined over the years as I helped young friends successfully get through school. I call it the "overview system."

Have you ever tried to drive a car to a destination known only by name or address, with someone giving you staccato directions for each turn moments before you approach the corner? Compare that with a trip where you have looked over the entire route on a map first, and as you go along your guide gives you the same information.

A lot less stressful, isn't it? That's because you are aware of the total picture; you know where you are going and have at least a general idea of how to get there. You do not have to absorb entirely new information in a short time. Rather, you supplement what you already know and are much more receptive to this additional information.

To adapt this overview system to your law school studies, start by acquiring the required casebooks as early as you can before classes commence. At the same time, also buy the textbook specifically written to accompany each casebook. If you can't afford it, get it at the library. If you lay the textbook and casebook side by side, you will see that they complement each other. Most of the time, the cases in the casebook are referred to in the textbook.

When an author puts together a student casebook on a particular subject—contracts, for example—cases illustrative of specific legal principles are assembled in historical order to show the development of the subtopic at hand. Under the section heading "What Constitutes a Contract," the first case chosen for the casebook might perhaps be some old English, New York or other state opinion discussing the proposition that a purely social agreement does not rise to the status of a contract. The next case might be from some other jurisdiction, pointing out that an agreement against public policy is not legally enforceable as a contract. The opening sentences of the accompanying textbook, under a similar chapter heading, might read:

Not every agreement between two persons constitutes a contract. Thus, it has been held that an invitation to dinner is an agreement relating to a purely social arrangement, and as such is not actionable in a court of law. Likewise, a suit will not lie to collect a gambling debt in a jurisdiction where gambling is illegal, for the courts will refuse to enforce an agreement that is fundamentally against the expressed public policy of the state.

The textbook summarizes, along with many other cases, the holdings of the opinions in the casebook; the opinions in the casebook elaborate on the statements of the law found in the textbook.

In the casebook, the citation of the case appears at the beginning of the case. In the textbook, the citation appears in a footnote. In our hypothetical illustration, both books cite the same two cases. This generally parallels reality. When using your actual casebooks and accompanying textbooks, you will find that it is relatively easy to cross-reference the judicial opinions with the editor's text.

To use the study method I suggest: First, without trying to learn anything, and going as rapidly as you can, copy the textbook sentence giving the holding of the case on top of the title of the case in the casebook. Do this for every case in the casebook. At this stage you are not trying to learn anything, only doing mechanical copying. The purpose of all this is so that you will have the rule of the case right in front of you when you later start to study.

Should there be no textbook specifically designed to accompany a particular casebook, use another available one to get as many of these one-sentence holdings as you can. A number of the cases are standard fare, and a prior edition by the same author, or even by someone else, may have many of the same references. To save time, you may have to skip a few of the missing cases for the time being. Later, if you feel it is necessary, you can look up those cases in the digests or the reports and pick out what seems to be the most applicable headnote to fit the particular place in the casebook table of contents under which the case has been categorized. But if you do this, make some note to remind you that it is a headnote you picked and that it may not be the holding you are looking for.

Probably without realizing it, by putting down the rule of the case (what the case holds; what it stands for) for practically every case in the casebook, you will have actually read the textbook through once and have also written it once before school has even started. Although you were going rapidly without trying to make or retain meaning from what you were doing, at the very least you have been subconsciously exposed to the contents, and you may have picked up a bit more than you expected.

It could take the better part of two weeks to do this rule copying for all your first-semester courses, depending on how fast you can go and how continuously you work. If you do not finish before school starts, try to be equally far into each casebook so that you will be ahead in every course. The more you can complete in advance, the more time you will have to study during the semester.

Next, study the table of contents of each casebook. Look up all unfamiliar table terms in your law dictionary and write the definitions on top of each word. Do not guess; if a word looks like it is a legal term, look it up and write it down. You do not have to make any attempt to memorize these definitions at this time; the main thing is to understand what you are reading at the moment. Later, through usage and reading the cases, these words will become an integral part of your vocabulary. Do memorize in advance, however, the major section headings, and the subheadings for at least the first one or two subsections.

In the customary method of law school study, you are expected to use the cases as building blocks with which to build a structure: the law for that particular subject. When you first start out, if you lack the overview, your unfamiliarity with the language may make it hard to comprehend what any one "block" is all about. It will be even harder to visualize what the finished structure will look like. Even at the end of the course, some students have only a hazy outline of what should by that time be as clear as an architect's rendering. Many spend the week just before exams struggling to get that clear picture; many do not succeed—it is too late.

Avoid that situation. The time spent studying and memorizing the table of contents will quickly give you a beginning idea of the building you are trying to erect. It is like visualizing the skeleton framework of a skyscraper: the unity which holds the whole thing together. Knowing that it is there, and what it looks like, will give you a perception of what the goal of the course is. As the details are filled in through daily class work, the image will become clearer, and by the time the final exam approaches you can spend your review time going over a sharp, professional-looking picture, instead of having to go through the frustration of trying to imagine a hastily sketched drawing as a well-crafted oil or watercolor.

In the next chapter, you will see how this preliminary review is used to fit the cases you read into the framework of each course.

6

HOW TO STUDY FOR CLASS

Some law schools send their students casebook reading assignment schedules several weeks before classes start; in others, they are usually posted in the library, outside lecture halls, or are available at the faculty office. You are expected to be ready to discuss the assigned cases at the first lecture period. Obtain your lists as early as possible. Then set yourself a goal of getting at least three weeks ahead in every subject.

If you cannot obtain these schedules by the time you want to start studying, assume that the professors will cover every case in the order the cases appear in the casebook. Should some cases you have covered be skipped, your work will not have been wasted. You will have at least given yourself a little background in the subject which may make it easier for you to understand what is to come. And as soon as you know the actual assignments, you can shift over to that material and still have time to get ahead before school starts.

Before each lecture period, all students in the class are expected to study the same designated cases and be ready to orally report on and discuss fully each issue raised in the opinions. Instead of actually lecturing to the students, the professor uses the Socratic method of interrogation to probe the students' understanding of the material.

27

First, one of the students is called upon to give a synopsis ("give the brief of the case"). Then the professor questions that student and others, beginning with what the case at hand actually holds, to ensure that everyone understands what the court is saying. This is then superimposed on what has already been studied in previous lectures, and through various "what if" questions the students are exposed to whatever legal principles can be squeezed out of the case. After several cases have been covered in this manner, the probing moves on to possibilities that may be uncovered in the next few cases, and finally, at the end of the subsection, to how the law in this area is likely to change in the future. Generally whatever lecturing is done comes during these summations and discussions of trends.

What is the professor looking for when the student is called on to "give the brief of the case?" Essentially: What court wrote the opinion? When was it written? How did the case get to that court? (Did it come up on direct appeal, procedural matter, or by some other means?) What are the facts? What legal issue are the parties arguing about? What is the holding of the case? (What legal rule did the court apply to the facts in order to reach its decision?)

Most beginning students will prepare for class by carefully and intensively reading each assigned opinion fully only once, perhaps twice, diligently highlighting what looks important, and then writing some summary in a bound notebook in the event, as they see it, they are unlucky enough to be called upon to enlighten the class. They do not have time to read each case more than once or twice because ever since childhood they have been taught that the only way to prove they have done an assignment is to have something in writing to show the teacher. So most of their energy goes into writing their brief of the case instead of learning what the case is all about. As a result, they find that they have spent an hour or more on each case and have only a hazy conception of what they have read. In order to finish the assignment, they then move along to the next case, with the same result. Students using this kind of preparation often get the point of the case wrong, fail to see the pattern developing through the progression of the assigned cases, and fail to retain the new material presented.

There is a way to get greater depth out of the same amount of study time. It is based on a lot more reading and a lot less writing.

When you finish a case you will have it all in your head instead of your notebook. When you get to class you will not be worried about getting called on; you will be able to constructively criticize the other students' presentations; you will be able to intelligently discuss the case, and you will not readily forget either the facts or the holding. At exam time you will have a strong understanding of the course and will have the confidence you need to do well.

As you get into the briefing of these cases, keep in mind that they are the appellate decisions of trial court cases that have been appealed by the losing party. The trial court has determined the facts. The appellate court is generally limited to those facts and does not reach an independent conclusion as to what they are. It assumes the facts, as found, to be true, and then goes on to apply the law as it perceives it to that specific set of facts. Compare an appeal to a box with items in it. If the facts are not in the box, the appellate court cannot get to them. It does not hear any witnesses; it is bound by the written record sent up to it by the court below.

Frequently, law students are troubled because they refuse to accept this convention; they are concerned about how the appellate court knows these are the true facts. For example, when the crucial point is a dispute about what one person said to another when they were alone together, students will wonder how the appellate court knows who is telling the truth. They fail to realize that the lower court has already decided that issue, and that the appellate court has to respect that finding when it prepares its opinion.

When you begin to read an assigned opinion, close your yellow marking pencil and your notebook, and put your pen down. About the only time you will need to write anything as you work over the case is on the first reading, when you write the definitions of any new words or phrases you have looked up in your legal dictionary, right between the lines over the printed words in the casebook.

Start out reading as fast as you can. Go through the case five or six times, fast. Get the feel of it. Who is fighting? What are the facts? What is the argument all about? Try to visualize the incident so you can describe it to someone else in simple terms: Mrs. O'Leary's cow kicked over a lantern in the shed that started a fire which spread and burned down Mr. Jones's house eight blocks away. Now Jones is suing her for *damages* and she's arguing that (1) she's not responsible

29

for something that all cows do, and (2) even if she is, if the fire were next door, O.K., but eight blocks is too far away to make her pay, in any event.

Now, begin reading more slowly. Look at the rule of the case, written over the citation heading in the casebook, that you mechanically copied from the textbook before school started. As you intensely read the case five or six more times, you will begin to get a full understanding of the legal reasoning the court used to apply this rule to the facts of this case. Notice how the application of the rule is based on the previous cases you have studied in this subsection of the casebook. Think up some hypothetical situations to test the application of the rule: Suppose Mrs. O'Leary's next door neighbor was illegally keeping explosives in his barn and that is why the fire spread so fast; suppose Jones's neighbor had maliciously damaged the volunteer fire department pumper so water could not get to the roof. Try to predict what kind of factual situation may show up in the next case that could extend the application of the rule even further. Once you feel you understand the case and know why it is there and how it illustrates the development of the law up to that point, quickly read it over again a few more times to solidify your conception.

As you do this repetitive reading, you will find that the points in the case start jumping off the page at you. You will see things you did not notice on the first or second slow time around that suddenly make whole sentences in the opinion extremely clear. By the time you come to class you will be almost as familiar with the case as the professor. At the very least, you will be one of the few students in the class who can carry on an intelligent discussion about it.

By this time, you are probably wondering when you are supposed to start writing something down so you can remember all the material you have just gone over so intensely. Right now. But you do not have to put anything in a notebook.

Use the margin of the case book as a memo pad. That way everything will be close together when you review. Most of the time you will not need to write any words. Instead, all you need use are simple kindergarten stick figures to draw something to represent the facts. (The rule of the case is already written at the top of the page.)

For the cow-fire case, you might want to draw a circle with two horns on top, a couple of dots for eyes and a curved line inside for a smile to represent the cow's face, perhaps a straight line with a tail, a half-circle underneath with some lines for udders, and four legs for the rest of the body. Have one of the legs kicking over something that looks like it has fire coming out of it. Then put a string of dots over to a stick representation of a house that also looks like it is on fire. If you feel it will help, write "O'Leary" on the cow. "Jones" on the house, and "8 Blocks" on the dots. The rule of the case and this simple picture, coupled with your repeated readings, will give you almost total recall for class or future review.

Do not shortchange yourself on the number of times you read the case. You must spend as much time doing this as you would if you were briefing the case in the customary way.

Try it both ways and you will see how much more you understand and remember through this method. As you gain more experience, you will discover that you absorb the material much faster by reading many times, and that you take longer if you read the case only one or two times, highlighting with your yellow pen and trying to write something meaningful in your bound notebook.

Under my suggested study system, you do not read the opinion to find out what the rule of the case is (it is already written at the top of the page); rather, you read it to determine how the court logically reached the rule, how it applied it to the facts of the case, and why it is the next step in the development of the law in this area. As you gain more experience reading the cases, you will soon be able to figure the rule out yourself. You will be using the textbook solution primarily as a check against your conclusion. With this in mind, you should nevertheless still do this preliminary rule writing in the upper margin for every case in the book. It will remain valuable as a quick entry into the case and, when coupled with the stick picture, as a mnemonic aid in reviewing the course.

Under this method of study, you remember the work because you get a full understanding of each case as you are doing it; you see how it fits in with the cases before and after it; you understand why it represents a particular stage in the development of the law; you have tested it against your own hypothetical examples; you have explored how it might be applied in the future; and you have even done your own little bit of artwork to give you an additional memory jog.

Do not take notes on what the students say in class. Much of it will probably be wrong anyway, and it may mislead you if you refer to it in your review. Always, however, take down what the professor says. Frequently, during the course of the period, the professor will cite some other case that is not in the casebook. *Copy the citation down and read the case.* Do not forget that your casebook contains only the cases the editor found and decided to use. Also, any cases that came down after the book was published could not possibly be in it. Be careful to get everything relating to explanations of principles, summations of subtopics, and predictions of trends. The outside case references and these observations frequently show up on exams.

Many students have problems during the first few months of law school because they do not fully comprehend what either the judges or the professors are saying. Much of the difficulty comes because they assume they know what each of the words in the cases means, without stopping to consider that a number of them may be used in an unfamiliar way. Part of learning the law is learning its language. Words are the tools of the lawyer. Until you really learn how to use them in legal context, you will only be a mediocre laborer in the vineyard of the law.

Get yourself a good legal dictionary as early as possible. This is a must. Several standard one-volume works are available. Look at each of them and choose the one that seems easiest to use. Purchase one with a durable binding; you will use this book often in your professional career.

The legal dictionary differs from the regular dictionary in that it gives the meaning of words and phrases cited to cases where they were defined—where appellate courts have said that is what the words connote in a given legal context. You do not have to worry if you have never studied Latin, as everything you might come across in a case will be clearly translated and explained in the dictionary. If you are in court and the judge uses some phraseology which is unfamiliar to you, do not hide your ignorance; ask for its meaning, and undoubtedly it will readily be given.

If you have a question in class, no matter how elementary or stupid you might think it sounds, do not hesitate to ask it. Many times some small misconception may prevent understanding, but when it is removed everything suddenly becomes meaningful. If you are afraid the other students will laugh at your ignorance, remember that many of them do not understand what is going on either, but do not have the fortitude to get answers to their questions. You are in law school to learn. If it gives them pleasure to laugh at you, your better final grades will give you the last laugh.

7

HOW TO READ A CASE

Are you wondering what an actual case looks like? Here is one, *Booth v. Merriam et al*, 155 Mass. 521 (1892), taken from the official Massachusetts reports. It is typical of what can be found in any casebook on torts. Let us see what we can do with it.

For a very profitable experiment, after you have read this book through once, come back to this chapter for about an hour and actually work this case as if you were getting ready for one of your classes. That way, you will know whether my suggested method of study is suitable for you, whether you can modify it successfully to fit your personal reading habits, or whether you should use only part of it or none at all. At the very least, use this case to think about what system you will be using when you sit down to prepare for your first day of class. Do not wait until you have bought your books and are facing your first assignment. If you do, you will find yourself living the old Pennsylvania Dutch motto: "The hurrieder I go, the behinder I get."

When you return to this material to try out the study method, assume that you have looked up *Booth* v. *Merriam* in the accompanying textbook and have found this to be the rule of the case:

A landlord is not liable to the tenant for an injury caused by an overt or readily determinable defect in the premises.

I have left room so you can write this sentence in the space over the name and citation of the case that follows. Copy it now.

Let us also assume that on the first fast read-through you have looked up the following unfamiliar terms in your law dictionary:

et al.: "and others" (because of space limitations, normally only the name of the first listed party on each side is given).
suffered: permitted.
Mason, C. J: Chief Judge of the county court where this case was tried.
parole lease: oral rental agreement.
alleged exceptions: claimed objections to the ruling of the trial court.
Knowlton, J: a Justice of the Supreme Court, writer of the opinion.
implied covenant: an agreement which the law imposes on the parties to a contract, even though not considered by them.
caveat emptor: "let the buyer beware."
ubi supra: "where above mentioned" (previous citation).
exceptions overruled: trial court verdict stands (plaintiff's objections raised as grounds for appeal are without merit).

Copy these definitions now, abbreviated but discernible, over the applicable words in the text of the opinion. Then read the entire case over again four or five times, fast. Write the rule of the case here:

BOOTH v. MERRIAM *et al.*
Supreme Judicial Court of Massachusetts
155 Mass. 521 (1892)

TORT, for personal injuries occasioned to the plaintiff by falling into a cesspool upon land of the *defendants,* negligently suffered by them to be out of repair.

At the trial in the Superior Court, before *Mason,* C.J., there was evidence tending to show that the defendants were the owners of the house numbered 29 on Harvard Street in Boston, which set back from the street fifty or sixty feet, and of a yard in front of the house, and also another yard in the rear of the house; that the plaintiff's son, acting for his mother, hired the house of the defendant's agent, by a parole lease at a monthly rent, about three months before the time of the said accident, and the plaintiff had lived therein for these three months, carrying on the business of keeping boarders; that when the house was hired nothing was said about any yard, either in front or in the rear of the same; that the front yard was used to gain access to the house, and also to three or four other houses; that the yard in the rear was apparently designed only to be used by those occupying said house No. 29; that the cesspool was situated in the yard back of the house, and was used as a receptacle of the water that ran from the sink in the house, and was covered by a wooden frame, into which was set an iron cover; that the plaintiff, on the day of the accident, went out of the back door of said house, and started to go to a tub, which was placed under a window at the rear of said house, for the purpose of putting a piece of meat under the tub, this being where the plaintiff kept her meat; and that in walking from the back door towards the tub she stepped upon the iron cover, which was on a level with the surface of the ground, when it suddenly fell, causing the plaintiff to fall into the cesspool, and injuring her severely.

The evidence tended to show that the plaintiff did not know anything about the location of the cesspool, nor the manner in which it was covered, and that she did not notice anything about it at the time; that the wooden frame in which the iron cover was placed had become so badly decayed as to be incapable of holding any weight; and the plaintiff contended, upon the evidence, that it must have been in the same condition at the time when said house was hired as aforesaid. No question was made that the plaintiff did not exercise due care.

Upon the evidence, the judge ruled that the defendants would not be

37

liable to the plaintiff in this action, and that the action could not be maintained.

The jury returned a verdict for the defendants; and the plaintiff alleged *exceptions*.

KNOWLTON, J. In an ordinary lease of a dwelling-house there is no implied covenant that the premises are in good repair or fit for habitation. "The rule of *caveat emptor* applies, and it is for the lessee to make the examination necessary to determine whether the premises he hires are safe, and adapted to the purpose for which they are hired." *Cowen* v. *Sunderland*, 145 Mass. 363, *Stevens* v. *Pierce*, 151 Mass. 207. If there is a concealed defect that renders the premises dangerous which the tenant cannot discover by the exercise of reasonable diligence, of which the landlord has or ought to have knowledge, it is the landlord's duty to disclose it, and he is liable for an injury which results from his concealment of it. *Cowen* v. *Sunderland, ubi supra. Minor* v. *Sharon*, 112 Mass. 477. *Bowe* v. *Hunking*, 135 Mass. 380.

The plaintiff contends that this case shows the existence of such a defect, and that it is like *Cowen* v. *Sunderland*, in which it appeared that there was a cesspool covered with decayed boards and earth four to six inches deep, on which grass and weeds were growing, in a yard hired by the plaintiff, and that it had been repaired with old boards some time before by the defendant's direction. The case at bar differs from that in important particulars. There was an iron cover set in a wooden frame which covered the cesspool, and was level with the surface of the ground, thereby disclosing to everybody that there was a covered excavation there designed for use. The accident happened solely because the frame was old and out of repair, and there is nothing to show that its condition was not easily discoverable on examination, or that the defendant had actual knowledge of its condition, or was culpably responsible for it. It was as much the duty of the plaintiff, when she hired the house and yard, to examine the premises and ascertain whether they were in such repair that she could safely use them, as of the defendant. The case is similar to *Bowe* v. *Hunking, ubi supra*, and it falls within the general rule that a tenant cannot recover for an injury received by reason of the want of repair of the premises hired.

Exceptions overruled.

Having done your fast readings, do you understand what happened; why the parties are in court; who won down below?

Mrs. Booth rented a dwelling house from Merriam on a month-to-month basis. There was no written lease, just a verbal agreement. Nothing was said about the condition of the premises. Some months later, as she walked through the yard, she stepped on a cesspool cover with a weak frame. There was no evidence to indicate that the landlord was aware of the condition. The boards broke and she fell in and was injured. She sued Merriam for damages.

Based on this set of facts, the trial judge ruled that she did not have legal grounds to hold the defendant liable and directed the jury to find for the defense. Now she is appealing to a higher court.

When you have actually gone back and are doing your experimental analysis of this case, do not read any further than the end of this paragraph, but instead, read the opinion through slowly four or five times to grasp the legal arguments of the parties and to see how and why the appellate court resolved the issue as it did. Only after you have done that slow, intensive rereading should you move on to my following comments.

You will observe that appellant, Mrs. Booth, is contending (by her lawyer through the briefs and oral argument) that the landlord had a duty to warn her of the dangerous condition of the cesspool cover. She concedes that under the general rule a tenant normally cannot recover damages from the landlord for an injury occurring because the premises need repairs; however, she argues that in this case the rule should not be applied because the facts bring her case under an exception to the general rule: allowing recovery if there is a *hidden* defect in the premises which the landlord knew or should have known about.

The court compares the facts in the cases she cites with those in the case at hand and concludes that this is not a hidden-defect case. It suggests that the tenant had as much a duty to inspect the premises as the landlord, and since the evidence does not indicate that either had done so, it will not presume any advantage to the tenant. The court iterates the general rule, and by this case refines it slightly, holding: a landlord is not liable to the tenant for an injury caused by an overt or readily determinable defect in the premises.

Did you notice as you worked through this case that the court has given us a little history of the development of the law in this area? We learn that the tenant takes the premises as is; that he or she should make a personal inspection to see if there is any dangerous condition; that without any agreement between the parties, the landlord is under no duty to search for defects; that if the landlord knows or is chargeable with knowledge of any hidden defects (maybe he caused some bad construction or repairs to be made), then the landlord has a legal duty to bring this to the attention of the tenant.

By the time you would actually reach this case in the casebook, you would have learned that among the elements of a tort action which the plaintiff must prove in order to win is that the defendant owed the plaintiff some legal duty and that the breach of that duty caused the injury.

In the *Booth* case, the Massachusetts court found that Merriam was under no legal duty to notify Mrs. Booth of the defect in the cesspool cover. Consequently, it did not have to go any further in order to find there was no liability.

Well, you have gone through this case fairly intensely. Can we try our knowledge on a couple of *hypotheticals*? Suppose the original oral lease had been in writing? Suppose the lease said the building could only be used as a single-family dwelling? Suppose Booth had asked Merriam to fix the cover and he agreed to do so, but had not gotten around to doing it at the time of the accident? What if, under that circumstance, one of Booth's boarders fell in? How about some neighbor's child taking a short cut through the yard? What about a night burglar?

We forgot to draw the stick picture to further identify the case. Although this was a cesspool, I mentally connect it with an outhouse, and to me, it will always be the outhouse case. My drawing is a door with a crescent moon near the top, adjacent to a wavy line representing the water level in the cesspool. Sticking out of the water is a circle with curls on it and a frown in it, my conception of poor Mrs. Booth.

Give the case a name; create your own picture and draw it in the book now, right up next to the rule of the case you wrote when you started. It will be a long time before you forget *Booth* v. *Merriam*.

As you go through the cases in your casebook, be aware that many of them, like this one, do not necessarily represent the actual state of the law now. Rather, they are there to show the development of the law; to give you practice in judicial reasoning; to get you in the habit of using legal terminology as part of your thinking. Also remember that the holding in a case may later be changed by statute in the jurisdiction where it arose; that the law is not necessarily the same in every state; and that a federal constitutional issue, not perceived at the time, may be decided years later in a way that wipes out the effect of applicable past decisions.

8

THE IMPORTANCE
OF COMMON LAW

American law has its roots in the law of England, and our legal system is known as Anglo-American law. When the colonists arrived here they came as English citizens entitled to all the rights of Englishmen. Thus, they brought with them the legal structure of that country: its unwritten constitution, including the protections of the Magna Carta; the recognition of all unrepealed statutes of the realm; the system of trial and appellate courts; and, most important to us as law students, the legal principles enunciated and recorded in the opinions of the courts. These opinions, a great body of law much more voluminous than all the rest, form the basis of our studies. Collectively, these cases are referred to as the common law.

Today, we do not actually study very many of these old cases; occasionally we come across one, however, that is still a significant landmark. But there are now so many thousands of American cases to choose from that the casebook editor usually opts for cases that give a more modern flavor to the work. Our American cases are sometimes referred to as American common law.

One thing to keep in mind for when you may be writing a legal argument is that it is always proper to cite one of these old English cases, either for direct application of its principle, for use in analogical reasoning, or for historical enhancement of your position. American common law includes all of the law of England (constitutional, statutory and common) in existence immediately before July 4, 1776, when our Declaration of Independence was signed. Today, many common law principles, both English and American, have been enacted into topically organized statutes known as codes. And many states have express statutes providing that there are no common law crimes in those states.

Despite such statutory pronouncements, our courts will nevertheless look closely at common law principles and historical background in interpreting the meaning of current legislation. When I was a deputy attorney general handling prosecution appeals, I once used the common law to suggest overruling a felony conviction because the trial court result seemed unjust to me. (Many law students do not realize that the true function of a prosecuting attorney is not to try to win every case at any cost; rather, it should be only to use the law to insure that justice is enforced, totally within the limits of the system.) At early common law, it was no crime to eat a meal at an inn and not pay for it, as the supplying of food was considered a service, not something which could be the subject of theft. It was only after the Innkeepers Statute was passed by Parliament that such behavior became the crime of "defrauding an innkeeper." In my case, the defendant Fiene and two associates went into an all-night beanery, ordered steak and eggs, and tried to get out through the door adjacent to the back restroom without paying. As this was at least the second time this had happened, the suspicious chef was waiting outside with a meat cleaver.

When the three men were brought into the Municipal Court, the two associates pleaded guilty to petty theft and were each let off with twenty-five dollar fines. Unfortunately for Fiene, his record included a prior felony conviction, and as in California "petty theft with a prior" is in itself an independent felony, he was held over to answer to Superior Court. He was convicted at trial and was sentenced to a jail term.

This is what the typed decision on appeal looked like in the court file, before it was published in the reports as *People* v. *Fiene*, 226 Cal. App. 2d 305 (1964). I have included it for those of you who might wish to practice analyzing another actual case. Compare the modern usage of language by the court in this case with the archaic wording in *Booth* v. *Merriam*. Here is the rule of law to write at the top:

A SPECIAL STATUTE IS AN EXCEPTION TO A GENERAL STATUTE AND TAKES PRECEDENCE OVER IT.

In this case, the appellate court reversed a trial court conviction for the independent felony: commission of misdemeanor petty theft by a person previously convicted of another felony (petty theft with a prior.) Since there was an existing misdemeanor statute making it a crime to defraud an innkeeper, which had the same elements as the crime of petty theft, the appellate court applied the rule above. It concluded that the Innkeeper Statute was a special statute, and determined that was what Fiene should have been originally charged with, instead of petty theft. The special statute took precedence over the general statute.

Once that conclusion was reached, logic required the finding that since there was no statutory independent felony (defrauding an innkeeper by a person previously convicted of another felony, i.e. "defrauding an innkeeper with a prior" as compared with "petty theft with a prior"), Fiene was actually convicted of a felony that did not exist. Copy the rule here:

IN THE DISTRICT COURT OF APPEAL
OF THE STATE OF CALIFORNIA
SECOND APPELLATE DISTRICT
DIVISION FOUR

THE PEOPLE,
    Plaintiff and Respondent
             v.
VERNON EARL FIENE,
    Defendant and Appellant.

2d Crim 9225
FILED
April 18, 1964

APPEAL from a judgment of the Superior Court of Los Angeles County, Joseph L. Call, Judge. Reversed.

Prosecution for petty theft with a prior conviction of a felony. Judgment of conviction reversed.

Defendant was found guilty by the court of a violation of section 667 of the Penal Code, petty theft with a prior conviction of a felony. Probation was denied and defendant was sentenced to a county jail term. He appeals from the judgment of conviction. A resume of the facts is as follows:

On February 11, 1963 at about 3:00 A.M., defendant and two other men entered the Valley-Ho restaurant and ordered meals. After eating, defendant got up, went to the restroom for a few minutes, and then left the restaurant by the side exit. One of the two remaining men asked for and was given the check for the price of the meals. Approximately ten minutes after the defendant had left, the other two men started for the restroom, and then left by the same exit defendant had used. No one paid the check in the amount of about eight dollars. The manager saw the two men leave and followed them outside. When he yelled at them, one of the men took off running. He then saw the defendant standing behind a station wagon in the parking lot. When he shouted to some of his customers, who had emerged from the restaurant, asking that they get the police, defendant and the other man also ran off.

Two or three weeks prior to this episode a similar incident took place at the same restaurant. Defendant and the first man to run, had come in, ordered meals and left without paying for them. On that occasion, after eating, defendant went to the restroom, the other man followed shortly thereafter, and both left by the same side exit.

Defendant told an investigating police officer, who spoke to him at his home on the morning of the February 11 incident, that he had been home all night. However, he later told the same officer that he had been to the restaurant with the other two men, there had been no agreement as to who would pay; after eating he went to the restroom; he then left and walked home.

Defendant stated to another police officer that he had been drinking before he entered the restaurant; at the same time he entered he had only 25 cents on his person; the first man who had run, Weeder, was going to pay the check. When the officer later told the defendant that he had talked with Weeder, and Weeder denied even being in the restaurant that morning, defendant said, "Well, it wasn't Weeder that was going to pay the check. Some fellow in the next booth was going to pay. I don't know who he was." Defendant then said he had never seen the man in the next booth before.

At the trial, the People introduced records showing that defendant had two prior felony convictions and that he had served state prison terms as a result of each.

We find no merit in the sole contention raised by the defendant, namely that the evidence is insufficient to sustain the verdict. The rules declared in *People* v. *Newland*, 15 Cal. 2d 678, require that we make such a finding. However, the attorney general, with commendable objectivity, raises a much more serious question, one which is raised for the first time in these proceedings, and, one which, we believe, requires a reversal of the judgment.

The question presented is whether the existence of Penal Code section 537 (The Innkeeper Statute), making it a misdemeanor to defraud an innkeeper, prevents the superior court from acquiring jurisdiction in this matter.

Section 537 reads in part: Any person who obtains any food . . . at a hotel, inn, restaurant, . . . without paying therefor, with intent to defraud the proprietor or manager thereof . . . is guilty of a misdemeanor." Defendant was charged with and convicted of the crime of petty theft with a prior conviction of a felony. (Pen. Code. §667.) Section 484 of the Penal Code is the general statute defining theft. The value of the property taken in the instant case was well under the $200 limit for petty theft.

The rule is well established that where a general statute, standing alone, includes the same matter as a special statute, and thus conflicts with it, the special act is to be considered as an exception to the general statute, whether it was passed before or after the general enactment. (*In*

47

re Williamson, 43 Cal. 2d 651, 654; *People* v. *Swann,* 213 Cal. App. 2d 447, 449.) . . .

In the case of *In re Joiner,* 180 Cal. App. 2d 250, the defendant, after taking his automobile to a garage for repairs, later entered the premises of the garage after closing hours, and without permission, retook possession of the automobile. He was subsequently apprehended and charged with burglary and grand theft. The appellate court, relying on the rule stated in the case of *In re Williamson, supra,* held that the superior court was without subject matter jurisdiction to try the defendant because his conduct came within the provisions of a special statute, section 430 of the Vehicle Code, making it a misdemeanor for anyone by trick or device to take a vehicle held subject to a lien. (See also the recent case of *People* v. *Swann, supra,* decided by this court, wherein upon similar facts, the same rule was applied.) We feel that these cases are determinative in the instant case.

The judgment of conviction is reversed.

JEFFERSON, J.

We concur:

BURKE, P.J.

KINGSLEY, J.

You will see another example where the application of the common law was very important when we get to the chapters on Moot Court and appellate briefing.

9

WRESTLING AROUND
WITH THE WRITS

From almost your first day of law school you will hear about writs.
The writ was the first document filed in a lawsuit at common law. It
was issued to a prospective plaintiff, for a fee, by one of the king's
officials. The writ contained the names of the parties, a description
of what the contention was, and a direction to a sheriff to serve it on
the defendant and bring him into court. The plaintiff's lawyer
would give the writ to the sheriff with instructions regarding details
of service and pay the sheriff a designated fee plus an advance for
expenses.

The history of writs starts in 1066 A.D. That is the big date in
English law. In that year, King William of Normandy established his
legal right to the English throne by defeating King Harold at the
Battle of Hastings. After the victory, William divided the kingdom
among his supporters and introduced a method of government
known as the feudal system.

Feudalism was based on land ownership. Everyone in the kingdom owed allegiance to the king directly as well as through the
landowner one served. Serfs, a cut above slaves, were bound to the
land where they were born, and their allegiance was to the lord of
their manor and, through him, to the king. The landowner's alle-

giance was to the king and the noble directly over him, that noble's allegiance was also to the king and to the noble above him, and so on. This centralization of allegiance brought strong centralization of government. Laws operative throughout the realm were proclaimed in the king's name. Taxes were collected and funneled into the central treasury. A system of royal courts evolved for the settlement of disputes between subjects in civil matters, and for the settlement of criminal disputes between king and subject in criminal matters.

Initially, the judicial structure was located at the seat of government and was literally "the king's court." Cases were heard before the king and the assembled nobles, and the king, acting as judge, decided the results after discussion with the nobles. As business grew, however, the king gradually referred the cases to his chancellor for determination. A bureaucracy rapidly developed in the chancellor's office (*chancery*) as it became necessary to screen the requests for hearing to determine what kind of case it was, what was necessary to give the defendant an opportunity to present the other side, how much time it would take, and so on. After the details were determined, a writ was composed and the case commenced. Eventually, the litigants throughout the kingdom persuaded the king to establish a system of branch courts. Members of the chancellor's staff were appointed judges and went out on circuit to hear cases in the provinces. A group of expert lawyers gradually developed to handle the cases presented before the courts.

William Blackstone, the great early English law writer, gives an excellent description of the court structure, the bar and the various types of cases in his monumental treatise, *Commentaries on the Laws of England*. It would not hurt, if you have the time, to browse through it. You will obtain some good background, not only on the court structure but on much of the law school work in pleading, property, contracts, torts, and crimes. (Incidentally, after you are in law school a while, you might enjoy spending a little time in the library stacks rummaging through the older books on the shelves. Such exploratory browsing will not only broaden your legal understanding but will make you aware of social customs and practices which you never suspected existed so many years ago.)

The spread of the court system led to the proliferation of writs covering every type of controversy. By the latter half of the 13th century, to make their jobs easier, the writ clerks persuaded the chancellor to stop the issuance of new writs and force litigants to fit the facts of their cases to one of the writs used in the past.

Here is a hypothetical example of how the writ system operated.

De pipa vini carianda, an actual writ described in "Black's Law Dictionary," was a writ which covered the situation where a wine seller had engaged a person to transport his wine to a tavern in an adjacent town, and on the way, the "pipe," or container, broke, allowing the seller to sue the carrier. Because this writ had successfully stood up in court before the no-new-writ rule was adopted, it was on the list of known writs which could be used.

Let us suppose for a minute that six friends went into a tavern in those days, sat at a big, rough oaken table in the back near the fireplace, and ordered a round of drinks. In this place, the proprietor's custom was to put a big jug of wine on the table. As the friends drank, they poured their own. The proprietor charged them by the glass—he observed and noted with a charcoal mark over the fireplace each time a glass was filled. In the revelry, one of the friends dropped the container; the big jug cracked and the contents were transformed into a mournful stain on the floor. The proprietor demanded that the friends pay for the undrunk beverage at what he estimated was the per glass rate. They refused. He sued.

His lawyer could not find any writ to cover this kind of case. But perhaps a colleague in the profession remembered that in another shire, or county, a writ of *de pipa vini carianda* had successfully been brought some years previously. The old file copy of the writ was obtained, names were changed, and the lawyer argued that breaking a jug at a table, when you did not own it or the contents, was the same as breaking it in transit when you were delivering it from maker to tavern owner. If the court hearing the case agreed with the analogy, the writ would be granted. However, in this hypothetical case, the strict construction prevalent at that time undoubtedly would have resulted in a verdict for the defense. The facts did not fit the writ.

The prohibition on issuance of new writs eventually reached a compromise. The lawyers got the rules changed, and about eleven writs, covering almost every situation, came to be used most of the time. The eleven writs developed into what was known as "causes of action." In order to have a cause of action, the factual situation had to conform to certain principles, different for each type of cause. These principles became known as the *elements of a cause of action.*

Here is a list of the eleven common-law causes of action:

COVENANT: Action brought when a defendant failed to perform a contract under seal (a contract formalized by signature and a seal impressed in wax).

INDEBITATUS ASSUMPSIT: Action on an oral or written contract, not under seal, where the broken promise is implied from the terms of the contract.

SPECIAL ASSUMPSIT: Action on a contract, not under seal, where the defendant has breached a specific promise in the contract.

DEBT: Action to recover a specific sum of money, the amount being readily ascertainable.

TROVER: Action for damages where someone has unlawfully taken another's personal property.

REPLEVIN: Action to recover the personal property itself which was unlawfully taken.

DETINUE: Action to recover personal property originally rightfully possessed, but not returned when due, together with damages for the unlawful keeping.

ACCOUNT: Action on the balance of a series of transactions between the parties (sometimes called "common counts").

EJECTMENT: Action for recovery of land, together with damages for the unlawful possession.

TRESPASS: Action for damages for direct injury to the plaintiff.

TRESPASS ON THE CASE: Action for damages for indirect injury to the plaintiff (often referred to as "case").

Modern pleading does not use these common-law divisions of causes of action. However, it is still important to know of their existence, and to have some understanding of their meaning, to fully comprehend the present-day system of code pleading. A lawyer still has to include the modern elements of a cause of action in the complaint or the case will be dismissed.

10

THE PAPERS IN THE OLDER CASES

In order to give you background for modern law, you will be exposed to old cases which established turning points in the law. Without at least a rudimentary knowledge of the papers filed at the trial court level in the old days, you may get quite confused, for frequently these old decisions mixed procedure and substance in their analyses.

As we noted in the last chapter, the first document issued was the *writ*. It generally was lengthy and served two functions. It set out the facts of the plaintiff's complaint, and also directed the sheriff to serve it on the defendant and bring him before the court. To the writ was attached the plaintiff's *declaration*, which detailed the elements of the cause of action. Here is what an English writ of trespass for assault and battery looked like. This one is taken from *A Treatise on the Principles of Pleading in Civil Actions* by Henry John Stephen, published by Robert H. Small, of Philadelphia, in 1831. It is typical of the writs of trespass used for hundreds of years.

Before you read this writ, please do not think that this extremely archaic and complex language is typical of the material you will have to work with in law school. It definitely is not. I do not want to frighten you off before you even get started.

Here is what this writ is all about. Albert Bottom was beaten up by Charles Dawson. Bottom then started a lawsuit against Dawson for damages. The first thing his lawyer did was to go to the court clerk's office, pay the necessary fee and obtain this writ. It was then given to the sheriff for service on Dawson. The writ directs the sheriff, provided that Bottom puts up a bond and security for costs ("gages and safe pledges"), to arrest Dawson and bring him before the court, wherever it happens to be sitting at the time, two days after Halloween (the morrow of All Souls) to answer the charges and show why he should not pay Bottom damages.

George the Fourth, by the Grace of God, of the United Kingdom of Great Britain and Ireland, King, Defender of the Faith, to the Sheriff of Nottingham, greeting:

If Albert Bottom shall make you secure of prosecuting his claim, then put by gages and safe pledges, Charles Dawson, late of Kentbury, yeoman, that he be brought before us on the morrow of All Souls, wheresoever we shall then be in England, *to show wherefore, with force and arms*, at Kentbury aforesaid, *he made an assault upon the said Albert Bottom and beat, wounded, and ill-treated him, so that his life was despaired of, and other wrongs to him then there did, to the damage of the said Albert Bottom, and against our peace;* and have you there the names of the pledges and this writ.

Witness ourself, at Westminster, the 14th day of April in the 3rd year of our reign.

Signed, etc.

When Dawson was served with the writ, he was arrested and was held in jail until the time the sheriff produced him before the court, unless he could put up bail to guarantee his appearance. He was also served with Bottom's declaration, which looked like this:

In the King's Bench.

All Souls Term, in the 3rd year of the reign of King George the Fourth.

On August 4, 1823 to wit, Charles Dawson was attached to answer Albert Bottom of a plea, wherefore he the said Charles Dawson with force and arms, at Kentbury in the County of Nottingham made an assault upon the said Albert Bottom and beat, wounded and ill-treated him, so that his life was despaired of, and other wrongs to him there did, to the damage of said Albert Bottom and against the peace of our Lord the now King.

And thereupon the said Albert Bottom, by Warren Tompson his attorney, *complains:* For that the *said Charles Dawson* heretofore, to wit, on the fourth day of April in the year of our Lord One Thousand Eight Hundred and Twenty-three, *with force and arms,* at Kentbury aforesaid, in the county aforesaid, *made an assault upon the said Albert Bottom,* and then and there beat, wounded and ill-treated him, so that his life was despaired of, and other wrongs to the said Albert Bottom, then and there did; against the peace of our said Lord the King, and *to the damage of the said Albert Bottom of One Thousand Pounds, 1000 £;* and therefore he brings his suit, wherefore he prays judgment, and his damages by him sustained, by reason of the committing of said trespasses, to be adjudged to him.

Signed, etc.

The defendant had to reply to the writ and declaration if he wished to defend the case. If a plaintiff lost the case and could not pay the amount due as set forth in the defendant's bill of costs, the plaintiff was arrested.

Here is an interesting entry from the record of the Court of Chancery in the sixteenth century which I came across while browsing through Monro's *Acta Cancellarie,* published by William Benning and Co. of London in 1847. (Do not let the fancy title throw you— the whole book is printed in English.)

Geldard v. *Gardyner,* 12 Feb. 1596.

Forasmuch *as the plaintiff is so poor, that he is not able to pay the costs* for an insufficient bill for which an attachment went forth against him, *and therefore was appointed to be whipped; and for that, instead of whipping, the said plaintiff hath stood upon the pillory;* it is ordered by the Lord Keeper that the costs and the said contempt be clearly discharged, and that a Supersedes as be awarded for that purpose; but if he vex any more in this sort in forma pauperis [the court had granted him permission to sue without putting up any fees because he was a pauper], *then he shall, at the next time, be whipped.*

Occasionally, the courts showed greater compassion, as Monro indicates, with this order issued in *Dunyell* v. *Jackson,* November 17, 1575:

Whereas the matter in variance between the said parties was the 5th of this month, dismissed for such causes as are in the said order expressed, and the plaintiff adjudged thereby to pay the defendant 30s. costs; forasmuch as the *plaintiff being a very poor boy, in very simple clothes and bare-legged, and under the age of twelve years, came this present day into this Court, and desired that he might be discharged of his said costs;* it is, therefore, in consideration, *as well of his age, as also of his poverty and simplicity,* ORDERED THAT (upon an affidavit made that he is the same Laurence Dunyell named plaintiff herein) *he be discharged of the said 30s. costs,* and no process to issue out against him for the same.

With respect to pleadings in the old cases, generally the defendant had several options. He could deny the allegations in a *traverse* and plead what was known as "the general issue" (ask for a jury trial), or he could respond by making a technical objection to the declaration in the form of a *demurrer,* a *plea in bar,* or a *plea in abatement.* You may come across references to these in your first year of law school. A demurrer admitted the facts alleged in the declaration to be true, but argued that the declaration nevertheless failed to state a cause of action. Other pleas might be that the plaintiff lacked legal capacity to sue (plea in bar) or that there was a similar action then pending between the same parties (plea in abatement.)

If the defendant's technical objection was upheld, the plaintiff had to file a second pleading and the process was repeated. Eventually, the various pleadings resulted in an issue being reached on which the case was tried.

The lineup of the pleadings in the old cases looked like this:

Plaintiff	*Defendant*
Writ and declaration	Plea of General Issue (Traverse), demurrer, or other technical plea
Replication	*Rejoinder*
Surrejoinder	*Rebutter*
Surrebutter	

Inasmuch as the purpose of common-law pleading was either to reach an issue of law which the court could decide based on admitted facts, or an issue of fact (to be proven at trial) which the court could decide based on applicable law, the subsequent pleadings after the declaration and demurrer normally got shorter and shorter. Most of the cases never got further than the replication—rejoinder stage. Accordingly, the judges got rather testy if a lawyer made the pleadings too lengthy or padded them with scurrilous allegations. Monro cites several cases where verbose and libelous pleaders were rigidly disciplined to teach them not to repeat their performances. *Mylward* v. *Weldon*, February 15, 1596, is one of the most interesting and unusual ones:

Forasmuch as it now appeared to this Court, by a report made by the now Lord Keeper (being then Master of the Rolls), upon consideration had of the plaintiff's replication, . . . *that the said replication doth amount to six score sheets of paper and yet all the matter thereof which is pertinent might have been well contrived in sixteen sheets of paper,* wherefore the plaintiff was appointed to be examined to find out who drew the same replication, and by whose advice it was done, to the end that the offender might, for example sake, not only be punished, but also be fined to Her Majesty for that offence; and that the defendant might have his charges sustained thereby; . . . *and for that it now appeared to His Lordship, by the confession of Richard Mylward, alias Alexander the plaintiff's son, that he the said Richard himself, did both draw, devise, and engross the same replication;* and because His Lordship is of the opinion that *such an abuse is not to be tolerated,* proceeding of a malicious purpose to increase the defendant's charge, and being fraught with much impertinent matter not fit for this Court; *it is therefore ordered, that the Warden of the Fleet shall take the said Richard Mylward, alias Alexander, into his custody, and shall bring him into Westminster Hall,* on Saturday next, about ten of the clock in the forenoon, *and then and there shall cut a hole in the myddest of the same engrossed replication* (which is delivered unto him for that purpose) *and put the said Richard's head through the same hole, and so let the same replication hang about his shoulders, with the written side outward; and then, the same so hanging, shall lead the same Richard, bare headed and bare faced, round about Westminster Hall, whilst the Courts are sitting, and shall show him at the bar of every one of the three Courts within the Hall,* and shall take him back again to the Fleet, and keep him prisoner, until he shall have paid 10 £. to her Majesty for a fine, and 20 nobles to the defendant, for his costs in respect of the aforesaid abuse,

59

which fine and costs are now adjudged and imposed upon him by this Court, for the abuse aforesaid.

Moral: Keep it short or we'll wrap it around your neck.

Besides the common law there was another body of law which grew up, called *equity*. Equity courts stepped in where common law left off. Where money damages were inadequate as a remedy, equity could act. Thus, if one individual illegally drained waters over another's land, common law courts could give only money damages for the unlawful act. Equity courts, however, could issue an order to actually stop the improper drainage and to prevent it from happening again in the future. Noncompliance would result in imprisonment for contempt of court. A separate body of legal principles based on precedence was developed through the decisions of the equity courts. These courts were also under the jurisdiction of the king's chancellor. They were called courts of chancery. Instead of calling the parties "plaintiff" and "defendant," they were referred to as "petitioner" and "respondent."

With the development of modern statutory code pleading, both law and equity were frequently joined into one court system, and today, in most American jurisdictions, the county trial court can usually give whatever remedy is adequate and necessary under the facts presented. But again, as in common law, it is still important to have a knowledge of the basic principles of equity even though the specialized practice of the subject no longer exists. One of your law school courses will be entitled Equity.

11

JUSTICE WITHOUT JURIES

When we hear the word "trial," most of us imagine a courtroom with a judge sitting on the bench and twelve jurors sitting in the box deciding who will win the case.

The judge's function under modern law is to preside over the case and make rulings on the applicable law. The *jury*'s duty is limited to determining, through their verdict for the plaintiff or the defendant, what the facts are in the matter. If a jury has been waived by the parties, the judge then determines the facts and reaches the verdict.

Ruling on law includes determining questions of validity of pleadings (the papers filed by each side, such as complaint, demurrer, or answer); admissibility of evidence; propriety of questions asked witnesses by the lawyers; ruling on motions; and giving instructions to the jury so that they understand their function and know how to perform their duties. Most people who have served on juries do not realize that the lawyers in the case draw up proposed instructions, and after a conference with these lawyers, the judge decides which instructions to give.

Determination of facts is done by evaluation of testimony of witnesses and analysis of evidence presented.

Great care is taken when a jury is picked to make sure that the jurors have no knowledge of either the parties or the facts of the case. If the judge has any connection with the parties or the lawyers, either by relationship or business dealings, he or she must disqualify (recuse) himself or herself and have another judge assigned to preside over the matter. The basic idea is to remove any possible bias or prejudice from the trial.

This was not always the way things were done. In the very early days of the common law there were two types of trials: *trial by ordeal* and *trial by oath* or compurgators.

Trial by ordeal was based on religious beliefs originating in tribal practices. It is hard for us to realize that, before the Norman conquest in 1066, what is now England was largely divided up among many little tribes, each controlling its own small territory. Their antecedents went back to ancient Norse and Germanic societies—Vikings, Danes, Angles, Saxons, Jutes—and customs which had continued for many years. Trial by ordeal was used primarily in criminal cases. Testimony was given against the accused. Denial of commission of the crime was made. The factual issue was settled through some form of torture. If the accused survived, acquittal resulted. Blackstone describes this form of trial in IV *Commentaries,* Chapter XXVII, page 342:

The most ancient species of trial was that by ordeal. . . . This was of two sorts, either fire-ordeal, or water-ordeal; the former being confined to persons of higher rank, the latter to the common people. Both of these might be performed by a deputy; but the principal was to answer for the success of the trial; the deputy only venturing some corporeal pain, for hire, or perhaps for friendship.

Fire-ordeal was performed either by taking up, in the hand, unhurt, a piece of red-hot iron, of one, two, or three pounds weight; or else by walking barefoot, and blindfold, over nine red-hot ploughshares, laid lengthwise at unequal distances; and if the party escaped being hurt, he was adjudged innocent; but if it happened otherwise, as without collusion it usually did, he was then condemned as guilty. However, by the latter method Queen Emma, the mother of Edward the Confessor, is mentioned to have cleared her character, when suspected of familiarity with Alwyn bishop of Winchester.

Water-ordeal was performed, either by plunging the bare arm up to the elbow in boiling water and escaping unhurt thereby; or by casting the person suspect into a river or pond of cold water; and if he floated therein without any action of swimming, it was deemed an evidence of his guilt; but if he sunk, he was acquitted.

The old colonial ducking stool, which you may have read about in grammar school, was a vestige of this ancient practice.

In civil cases, one of the ancient forms of trial was trial by oath, also known as trial by wager of oath, or trial by compurgators. The defendant came into court and denied the charge (usually that he owed money) under oath. Even if there was no other evidence, if he could bring to court twelve neighbors, called "compurgators," who swore that they believed him, the case was dismissed.

The Normans brought an interesting type of trial from the continent, *trial by battel*. Initially, the parties themselves battled hand to hand in front of the king and assembled dignitaries of the court. Later, the system was altered to permit first the defendant, and then the plaintiff, each to have a substitute do the fighting for them. Well-known knights hired themselves out as champions for litigants. Lawyers drew the pleadings; knights fought the "battel," generally one on each side. You are surely familiar with movie scenes where the king and his courtiers sit on a field and watch opposing knights fight each other. Occasionally, these jousts were lawsuits being tried before the court. The groups of knights who worked together were really the trial law firms of the day.

The overtones of this system still continue in England today, where lawyers called solicitors take care of the paperwork law, and lawyers called barristers actually go into court and try the cases. It is fun to speculate that perhaps when the Blue Medallion Knights helped some beautiful golden-tressed maiden confined to an isolated ivory tower by her cruel guardian, they were really just lawyers taking a case on a contingency basis, and if they won at the jousts, their firm got a percentage of her estate and the junior partner married the girl he had so successfully championed. I recall reading an article once which said that trial by battel, although not in use for several hundred years, was not really banned in England until the last part of the nineteenth century, when a clever litigant demanded that right. Before the case got to trial, however, Parliament hurriedly passed a statute limiting the form of all trials to judge, or judge-and-jury proceedings.

Another custom the Normans brought with them was used to decide boundary questions. The king's representative and twelve long-time property owners of the neighborhood, accompanied by the quarreling landowners, rode around the perimeter of the disputed area, listened to the explanations and arguments of the respective proprietors, and then reached a decision as to where the correct line was. We possibly get our twelve jurors from the occasional use of twelve boundary riders, or perhaps from the twelve compurgators; the lawyers from the knights combatant; and the judges from, first, the king, then later from the judges he appointed to travel the kingdom on a more regular basis.

If you read something on the life of Abraham Lincoln you will find that, in his day, the courts of the state went on periodic circuits, with judge and lawyers traveling around to try the cases coming up for the term. And as you study your cases for this period, you will find that a number of them raise procedural questions relating to the effects of events occurring during one term on a case tried at a later term. This was also true in the federal courts. Today, each United States Supreme Court justice is still considered the justice responsible for all matters in one of the appellate circuits.

Basically, the jury is a part of the "law," as opposed to the "equity" side of the justice process. This was true from ancient days when "law" covered criminal prosecutions and civil suits for money damages. The jury's determination of the facts concluded the case. (Keep in mind that, in any case where a jury trial is required, it may be waived if all parties agree [*stipulate*] to the waiver.)

On the equity side, a jury was not used unless the judge wanted it to make some factual determination for him. In those cases, however, the judge made the final determination of the result of the case. This is still true today. Equity matters are generally referred to as "proceedings." Today, a judge sitting without a jury issues various writs ordering people to do or refrain from doing certain things. Probate of wills and administration of *decedent estates*, trusts, and guardianships are all nonjury proceedings. Bankruptcy is another. One of the largest volume-generating nonjury areas is in the field of *administrative law*. More and more, our daily lives are governed by the rules, regulations and decisions of *administrative agencies*.

Suppose, for instance, a homeowner wants to convert her garage into another bedroom. The county planning officer says she cannot do it because of a particular interpretation of the zoning ordinance. Her appeals to the planning commission, and from there to the county Board of Supervisors, are administrative proceedings. Hearings are held where evidence is taken, legal arguments are made, and a decision is issued.

A police captain in a large city refuses to issue a permit to carry a gun to a store owner in the precinct. The owner appeals to the Police Commission. Administrative proceeding.

The State Board of Cosmetology wants to revoke the license of a beauty shop because the combs are used on different customers without being sanitized before each new use. Another administrative proceeding.

Underlying all administrative proceedings is the basic theme that the officials and bureaucrats, who have been delegated power to regulate certain activities by the legislative body of some level of government, should not be allowed to reign unchecked. The public protection against abuse of discretion is the administrative hearing and subsequent appeal to the courts.

An administrative agency may consist of one person (aided by supporting staff) whose decisions are final, such as the Secretary of the Interior or the Director of Motor Vehicles; or a group of people making up a board or commission, such as a State Board of Medical Examiners or a City Planning Council. Administrative agencies usually have only the power that the legislative body has delegated to them. If they act in excess of that power, they have exceeded their jurisdiction. These agencies customarily interpret and exercise their power by issuing rules and regulations governing their operations. Before these rules or regulations become final, an agency is generally required to give public notice of its intent to proclaim them and to hold a hearing permitting public input into the subject under consideration.

In the federal system, and in most states, a *petition* may be brought in court to prevent a rule or regulation taking effect. A writ may be issued setting a date for a court hearing and ordering the agency to refrain from effectuating the proposed change unless it can "show cause" why it should not do so. The agency files a document responding to the allegations of the writ; legal arguments are heard from both sides, and a decision is issued. This, too, is a nonjury proceeding.

If someone applies for a license and is turned down, a hearing may be provided for. It is always required if an agency wants to take away or interfere with some vested right.

The hearing privilege may be waived. The waiver can be express, or by default. That is, the individual may say, "I don't want a hearing," or may fail to apply for one in the manner and within the time required by the statutes of the jurisdiction.

Often, people will try to bypass some or all of the administrative procedural steps and go directly to court. This is normally not permitted because of the doctrine of *exhaustion of administrative remedies*. The courts do not want to be cluttered up with cases that really are not final.

Let us suppose that the holder of a physician's license is convicted of some crime involving illegal prescribing of narcotics. Under the procedure in this particular state, the secretary of the Board of Medical Examiners files an *accusation* against the doctor before the Board, setting forth the charges and requesting that the license be revoked. The licensee files a document denying the charges. The matter is set for a hearing before an administrative law judge who may be employed by the Board or assigned from an independent panel to hear the case. Evidence is presented by each side. After the hearing, the administrative law judge writes a proposed decision which is submitted to the Board for its approval. If the Board accepts it, this becomes the Board's final decision, which is then subject to appeal through the courts.

If the Board does not like the decision, it rejects it. Under that circumstance, in most jurisdictions, it may rehear the case itself; or it may read a copy of the reporter's transcript and study the physical and documentary evidence introduced at the hearing. It may then send the case back to the hearing officer with instructions to take additional evidence, or it may issue its own final decision. Because administrative proceedings may take quite some time, the licensee would probably try to get a court to issue a writ to the agency staying revocation of the license until the final decision has gone through the entire court appellate process.

In a criminal trial, the prosecutor's job is to convince judge or jury of the defendant's guilt "beyond a reasonable doubt." In civil cases, the *burden of proof* is on the plaintiff to convince the trier of fact by a "preponderance of the evidence." This burden is much lighter and means that there just has to be a little more evidence in favor of the plaintiff. Administrative proceedings are not criminal cases. The preponderance rule is applied. The burden of proof is on the applicant in a licensing case; it is on the agency in a revocation case. In these nonjury, administrative hearings, matters usually proceed much more informally than in regular court cases. Persons often represent themselves. The normal rules of evidence are relaxed, and hearsay evidence (testimony as to what someone who is not present said) is admitted.

If administrative law is only an elective course at your law school, take it anyway. It is an extremely important part of the volume of business in a big law firm, and can be extremely rewarding in an independent practice.

12

A QUICK LOOK AT FIRST-YEAR COURSES: CONTRACTS

The big four courses of first-year law school are contracts, torts, crimes, and property. Generally speaking, contracts covers the law applicable to individuals who enter into agreements with each other. Torts develops the liability for damages when one individual injures another, and crimes concerns prosecution of individuals by the government for violation of laws prohibiting certain conduct. Property covers land problems and the laws relating to ownership. In this and the next three chapters we will look at each of these subjects, without attempting a full analysis of any of them, to give you some idea of what to expect when you begin your studies.

Your first contact with contracts will possibly be through some obtuse old English cases which essentially boil down to the proposition that a contract is a legally enforceable agreement between two persons. There are some agreements, generally arising from social interactions, which courts will not raise to the dignity of contractual obligations. Suits based on them will usually be summarily dismissed without subjecting them to the customary tests to see if they have ripened into contracts.

Boy meets girl in the local supermarket. Because of their expressed mutual interest in the various brands of anchovies on display, she invites him over for the following Saturday night so together they can discover what makes the water from the whirlpool jets spin counterclockwise. He agrees to be there at seven-thirty with the proper colored wine for the occasion. If he does not show, can she sue him for the cost of the new bikini she has purchased, or the spectacular crab-stuffed steak she has prepared?

Anybody can sue anybody. The lawyer asks the question another way. Does she have a *cause of action* against him? (If she does sue, will a court say there are legal grounds for recovery of damages?) The answer here is probably no. The agreement to meet on a date is not one which the parties or society intended to be legally enforceable. (I used to answer that question with a categorical "no." But in 1990, I read a newspaper story that said some small claims court gave judgment in favor of a young girl who sued her prom date for standing her up. Of course, since it was not an appellate case, no new law on the point was created. But the law is constantly changing, and you may be reading this book a few years after its publication date. Who knows what level judicial wisdom might reach in the future?)

Change the facts a little. He is a professional photographer; she is a professional model. He asks her to meet him at a well-known spa so he can take some pictures for a fashion magazine. He has hired her before and knows what her customary fee is. It is mutually understood it will be paid. As an aside, both of them probably have visions of using the therapeutic watering facilities after the modeling session as the beginning of a very enjoyable evening (the "date" element.) In this case, however, if he does not show up, she has a valid cause of action against him for her fee. If she does not show up, he has a valid cause of action against her for his loss of time.

In the first example, the agreement to meet was just a social situation. In the second, there was a business agreement, which the law will enforce.

In reality, she may never sue him, or he may never sue her. That is not the point. When you are studying law, you are given factual examples to illustrate principles of law. You must learn to accept what is presented, isolate it, and apply the rule. Then you mentally change facts, add something new, and test the rule under different circumstances. It is extremely important to be constantly aware of this approach all through law school. You will often have some outside knowledge that will make it difficult for you to accept the factual situation presented in a case, or else your own practicality will make you ask, "How could anybody prove that actually occurred?" or "How could anyone do anything that stupid?" The best way to handle this problem is to think: Assuming the people really did act that way, what principle or rule of law is applied under those particular circumstances?

Although you may sometimes believe that the law is applied illogically, you will gradually realize that there is a logic to the way it has developed, and to the way in which the structure of each branch of law is built up, to make the totality viable and usable in everyday life. If you look a little closer at the elementary definition of a contract—"a legally enforceable agreement between two persons"— perhaps you will get a clearer idea of what I have in mind.

Focus on the word "persons". You normally would think it covers anybody, and not go any deeper than that. But the law says, "Wait a minute; there are different kinds of persons: men, married women, single women, senior citizens, children, idiots, the insane, prisoners, drunks, and so on. We are not going to let all these kinds of persons be bound by contracts. Public policy requires that we have special rules for special circumstances." All these persons can enter into agreements if they choose, but those agreements are legally enforceable only if they are contracts. Your contracts case book will have a section of cases setting forth the principle that, in order to have a contract, you must have parties capable of contracting.

At common law, married women could not enter into contracts; single adult women and widows could. A wife was considered one with her husband, and he was legally responsible for all the business activity of the marriage. Persons convicted of *felonies* lost all civil rights. Consequently, they too could not enter into contracts. People who were drunk, surprisingly, could, possibly because of the underlying community belief that they were personally responsible for getting into that state and therefore should suffer the consequences. Or perhaps it was because drunkenness was so prevalent that nobody thought of it as a legal disability.

71

The early common law recognized, however, that idiots did not have the mental capacity to enter into contracts. Senile people and insane people did not fare as well. Later on, however, the common law recognized that, if one of these individuals did enter into a contract which was grossly unfair, it could be set aside.

That leaves us with the children: persons who had not reached the age of 21 at common law. Many states have lowered the age by statute. Today they're called *minors*; the common law referred to them as *infants*. You will find a number of cases in your contracts book on the rules applicable to minors, and will probably also pick up some additional material on the subject in a course called "Persons." Basically, if you dealt with a minor, even though you were unaware of the fact of minority, you did so at your peril. A minor could enter into a contract with an adult, but only the adult was legally bound to perform. At any time during minority or for a short time after coming of age, the minor could get his money back by offering to return what he had received in the transaction. If the minor had used it up, the adult would still have to pay.

Seventeen-year-old Timothy Lithe, an energetic businessman, contracts with Robinson Broadbottom, an adult, to buy the peaches on Broadbottom's trees, payment to be made within ten days after the crop is picked. Tim and his crew do the picking, take the peaches to market, get the money. Tim pays off his crew and spends the rest of the money on the pleasures of life. Broadbottom sues for the contract price of the peaches. Tim pleads the defense of minority. Broadbottom loses the case and is left sitting on his name, lucky at least that he still has his trees.

Before the 1929 stock market crash, a minor who had started with a small amount of cash became a big operator almost overnight. He owed his broker a great deal of money. When the values plunged into the cellar, the stocks he held became practically worthless. When his broker sued him he alleged that he elected to rescind the contracts of purchase and offered to return all the stock certificates that were in his possession. The court decided it was time to modify the common-law rule. The minor lost the case. It was felt that the minor was an astute, knowledgeable investor, and that the basis of the old principle, the protection of minors from being taken advantage of by designing adults, was inappropriate under the circumstances of this particular case. Thus, a new rule was established: A minor may not disaffirm a stock purchase contract where he or she has essentially the same expertise as a seasoned trader in the market.

This is an example of how the law develops. A basic principle is established. From time to time exceptions are created. Sometimes the principle is totally changed by this erosive process.

Let us go back to our original definition of a contract: a legally enforceable agreement between two persons. We have looked at the "legally enforceable" and "persons" parts. Now we will zero in on "agreement."

The catchwords and phrases you will be immersed in are "offer," "acceptance," "consideration" and "public policy." This is one of the first places you will be exposed to the "or/ee" syndrome. Lawyers love to tack these syllables onto the ends of words just as the physicians toss out the "osises" and "itises." And so you will pick up new jargon like offeror/offeree, lienor/lienee, mortgagor/mortgagee, payor/payee, and donor/donee. The "or" ending indicates the actor or moving party in the situation: the one who initiates something causing someone else to react. The "ee" ending stands for the party on the other end, who gets whatever the "or" party is putting out. Thus, an offeror is a person making an offer; an offeree is the one to whom the offer is made. A purchaser of land gives a mortgage back to the seller for the balance of the purchase price. The purchaser is the mortgagor; the seller is the mortgagee.

You will probably have a lot of fun with give-and-take banter with other law students, bouncing this and other new language around and applying it to everyday situations as you try to make it a part of your thinking. Remember, though, that this activity is an "in joke" and, to the lay person, you may sound like a pompous idiot. Some lawyers never realize this. Even after law school they talk as if they have marbles in their mouths. Stuffy, boring, and pedantic, they put every social contact into some legal frame of reference, and have their listeners holding on to their wallets for fear of getting billed for the conversation.

You will learn that in every contract there is an offeror who makes an *offer* to an offeree. Before we can go any further, you will have to know what an offer is. You will run into a series of cases in your casebook giving various factual examples where courts found an offer either did or did not exist.

On April 16th, exhausted from the income tax rush, a tired accountant wails, "Oh, if somebody will just give me enough money to pay me what I paid for my office equipment, I'll sell out right now." Is this an offer to sell that a would-be buyer can hold him to?

An almost forgotten former movie star says, on meeting a group of her old fans, "My Oscar is for sale to the first person who gives me two hundred dollars." Is she making an offer to sell?

As you plow through the opinions, you will see a principle evolving to the end that an offer must directly or impliedly encompass an intended binding promise to do something if someone complies with the terms. The courts have to wrestle with factual interpretations revolving around the actual, implied or even apparent intent of the purported offeror. Historically, advertisements in newspapers describing merchandise and giving prices are not considered offers to sell, but are held to be in the nature of requests to the reading public to come into the store and make an offer to purchase at the price quoted. This common-law rule has been changed by statute in many states. You will learn that reward posters have been held to be offers; that there are all kind of rules for bidding at auctions; that there are numerous other situations where the existence of an offer is often arbitrarily determined by custom and usage in a particular area of commerce. Sometimes the conclusions seem strange; but when the rules of interpretation were first set down, the courts felt it necessary to have some certainty that people could rely on in their customary business dealings.

How long does an offer stay open? If you have what is known as an option, you actually have a contract to keep an offer open for a specific period of time. But suppose there is no option and the offeror or the offeree dies? Suppose the offer is revoked before acceptance? Suppose the offeree rejects the offer and then changes his or her mind? These are the kinds of problems you will run into in law school.

In order to effectively solve the problems you will be faced with in actual practice, you should start trying to think creatively early in your law school career. Once you are actually out handling matters for real clients, you should be able to apply old rules and adapt existing principles to new situations. The development of the law can be compared to crossing a river that does not have a bridge you can walk over. If it is too wide to jump, then look for stepping stones.

One of the interesting things you will observe as you take additional courses and learn new principles is that the theories of one course can often be carried over into another. Thus, for example, in torts you learn about the concept of the *reasonable man*, and in contracts you apply that idea to determine whether a reasonable man would really think certain language or conduct constituted an offer. This taking of ideas from other areas of the law greatly expands the analytical possibilities for solving problems. The greater variety of legal matters you are exposed to, the better lawyer you will become.

The law student learns to define, redefine, analyze into smaller pieces, split hairs, imagine eyelets on the ballet shoes worn by angels dancing on the heads of pins. And after all that, the student then has to apply principles and rules, either directly or by analogy, to the tiny part distilled out to see if an answer can be found to the problem presented. After several years of law school and practice, this intensive approach should become an almost mechanical thought process. While you will look at problems in much the same way after graduation, you will not realize you are doing so, and your solutions to new situations will start flowing more readily.

Another subject you will be exposed to in your contracts course, *acceptance*, reemphasizes the active analysis necessary to solve a legal problem. Look for different ways to consider whether a legally valid acceptance occurs. Are the parties talking about the same thing? In a very famous old English case, somebody insures a cargo on a ship: "ex Peerless, Bombay." During the journey, a violent storm destroys the vessel. It then develops that, outside the knowledge of either the insurance agent or the person insuring the cargo, there were two ships named Peerless sailing out of Bombay at about the same time. The insurance agent was thinking of one, the customer the other. The court held there was no valid acceptance, and consequently no contract, because there was no "meeting of the minds."

The offeree has to know of the existence of the offer before it can be accepted. Bleepo sends Curley a letter offering to sell Bleepo's prize bull for fifteen thousand dollars. Curley simultaneously sends Bleepo a letter offering to buy Bleepo's bull for fifteen thousand dollars. Held: There is no contract. *Cross offers* do not constitute an acceptance.

You probably are wondering what kind of crazy ruling is this. The parties have agreed on a price; they are talking about the same bull; and one wants to buy and one wants to sell. How come there is no contract? In the Bleepo bull case, several things might have happened to bring the matter to a lawsuit. Before Bleepo got Curley's letter, somebody may have offered Bleepo eighteen thousand dollars for the bull, and he sold it to that individual. When the third party found out Curley wanted it, that person offered to sell it to Curley for two thousand dollars more. Curley bought it and then felt that he was out of five thousand dollars. On the other hand, maybe when Bleepo got Curley's letter, he thought that if Curley wanted to pay fifteen thousand dollars, not knowing that Bleepo would sell for that amount, why, perhaps he would just raise the price a bit. Or maybe by the time Curley received Bleepo's letter he had already purchased a bull somewhere else.

You will run into a group of cases discussing the time an acceptance is made. Is it when the accepting answer is deposited in the mail box, or when it is actually received by the offeror? Suppose an offer is made by fax? What rules are applied when the acceptance is by fax, telephone, telegram, letter or in person?

Another major aspect of contracts is *consideration*. Every contract has to have consideration. The only exceptions at common law were contracts "under seal." That meant a written agreement was drawn up and signed by the parties, who also added the impression in wax made by their personal seal.

The easiest way to understand the meaning of consideration is not to think of it as money or something of value. Rather, think in terms of a unilateral (one-sided) or a bilateral (two-sided) contract.

In a unilateral contract, only one party is bound to do something. And that obligation arises only if the other party acts first in response to some offer. Boring says to Fitch, "Mow my lawn and I'll give you ten dollars." This is an offer to enter into a unilateral contract. At this point nobody is bound. Fitch is under no duty to mow; he can do so or not at his pleasure. If Boring revokes his offer before Fitch starts to mow, no contract arises. But if there is no revocation, and within a reasonable time Fitch does mow the lawn, Boring owes him ten dollars. Fitch's act of mowing in response to Boring's promise to pay creates a unilateral contract; the act is consideration for the promise.

In a bilateral contract, both parties are bound. A promise is given in exchange for a promise. Boring says to Fitch, "If you agree to mow my lawn by Tuesday, I'll give you ten dollars." Fitch says, "I'll be there no later than Tuesday, for sure." Here, there is a promise given in response to a promise: Boring promises to pay ten dollars in exchange for Fitch's promise to mow the lawn by Tuesday. Boring is bound to pay ten dollars when Fitch does the job. If Tuesday comes, and Fitch does not appear, there is a breach of contract. Boring can get someone else to do the job. If he has to pay more than ten dollars, Fitch is *liable* to Boring for the difference.

It is not enough, however, just to perform an act or make a promise in order to have valid consideration for a contract. You have to agree to do something, or to refrain from doing something that you do or do not legally have to do, and this doing or not doing must be the reason you give the promise. In a unilateral contract, the act performed in acceptance of the offer must meet the same criterion.

A busload of school children is hijacked and the governor of the state offers a $10,000 reward for information leading to the criminal's arrest and conviction. Carl Kopp, a detective in the county where the offense occurred, is assigned to the investigation. He finds the key clue that solves the case. Even though he knows about the reward and works extra hard hoping to collect it, he is not legally entitled to the money. He is just doing his regular job. He is under a legal duty to catch criminals. The reward is an offer to enter into a unilateral contract. The act which is performed in acceptance of the offer must be one which the acceptor is not legally required to do. Otherwise there is no consideration.

Walker tells his nephew he is giving him a five-hundred dollar watch for his birthday. The watch given is worth only ten dollars. The nephew had no cause of action against Walker because there was no consideration for the gift.

One of the things you have to look out for in consideration problems is whether the giving of the consideration itself is against public policy. Suppose A, a quiz-show contestant, promises to pay B, a television announcer, a sum of money if B will promise to give A the answer to the Magic Question on next week's show. B promises to do so, and actually gives A the correct answer. A wins but does not pay B. B has no cause of action against A. The consideration is tainted by illegality (the bribe) and fails. It is against public policy to use the law to perpetrate a fraud or enforce the commission of a crime.

In a state where betting is against public policy, A promises to pay B $50 if the Rams win by ten points next Sunday. B promises to pay A $50 if they don't. No enforceable contract. The consideration is illegal. Neither has a cause of action against the other.

This is the first time I have used "A" and "B" to distinguish the people involved. These appellations are helpful when you are trying to solidify your learning. Get used to them. Lawyers and judges use them all the time. They make it easier to apply abstract principles to different factual situations.

You will become familiar with a number of other rules relating to consideration. After you learn enough examples, you will be able to sense whether the consideration is valid or not. But for now, just be aware that, without it, you cannot have a binding contract.

Other aspects of the study of contracts include the Statute of Frauds (when a contract must be in writing); third-party beneficiary contracts (whether third persons, not parties to a contract but who stand to benefit from it, have any cause of action if one of the original parties does not perform as promised); what happens if one side fails to perform; when rights under a contract may be transferred or assigned; what is the legal status of the parties when they agree to cancel the contract and make a new one.

In recent years, almost all of the states have adopted the Uniform Commercial Code, a series of laws relating to commercial transactions such as contracts, sales of goods, bank checks, and other "negotiable instruments." These laws have taken many of the common-law rules which you will study in the cases and have put them together in a logical fashion, standardizing former majority and minority positions into one rule and making it easier for business people to deal with each other.

13

A QUICK LOOK AT FIRST-YEAR COURSES: TORTS

The course in torts covers the law applicable to wrongful acts to persons or property, by which others are injured or their property is damaged, and for which the law gives a remedy.

Before you can have a *tort*, there must be some underlying duty owed to the injured party. A man on shore sees somebody drowning. He can easily toss out a life preserver and save the other person's life, but he does nothing. The wife and children of the deceased sue him for wrongful death. No recovery. He was not under any legal duty to help, and although his conduct may have been morally reprehensible, it was not tortious. But suppose the man on shore was a lifeguard expressly hired to watch the swimmers off that beach. His inaction would probably constitute a breach of a legal duty owed to the man in the water, and a cause of action would lie in tort.

Everyone is under an implied legal duty not to injure anyone else. But the duty to give aid to another will arise only if certain specific legal relationships exist between the parties. You will be concerned with three broad areas of tort liability: intentional torts, negligent acts, and liability for inherently dangerous activity. All encompass some ramification of this concept that a duty must exist.

Obviously, an intentional act to injure another will be a breach of the duty not to injure owed to everyone. Among intentional torts are physical violence to the person (*assault* and *battery*), *false imprisonment*, invasion of privacy, malicious prosecution, fraud and deceit, libel and slander, *trespass*, and damage to or taking real or personal property. Generally, anytime some act that harms another person is done intentionally, a tort arises.

As a joke, A pulls a chair away just as B is going to sit down; B falls to the floor and is injured. This is an intentional tort. Even though no harm was intended, the act which caused the harm was purposely done. B has a cause of action against A.

Where there is an intent to injure, the trier of fact may also award punitive damages as punishment and as a deterrent to future conduct of the same nature. A collection agency employee knows Mrs. B is a pregnant widow with four children whose sole income is from her job as a secretary in a factory. She has been paying the agency fifteen dollars per month on some outstanding debts. The agency employee keeps calling Mrs. B at home at three A.M. every day demanding that she pay more and threatening to tell her boss that she is a deadbeat who should be fired. She gets so nervous from all this harassment that she has a miscarriage. This is a case where punitive damages could properly be awarded against the agency by the trier of fact.

Note that many intentional torts are also crimes. This means that, besides the individual victim, who has a civil cause of action against the perpetrator of the tort (the tort feasor), the State also has a criminal cause of action arising from the same set of facts. Two separate lawsuits could be filed: a privately brought one for money damages, and a publicly brought one which could lead to fine or imprisonment on conviction.

Most of your study of torts will be spent on *negligence* cases. First you will have to learn all the various elements which go to make up *actionable negligence*, and then you will have to know all the possible defenses.

In order to have a cause of action for negligence, there must be a duty of care owed to another; there must be a breach of that duty; the breach must be the *proximate cause* of some injury or damage; the

82

injury or damage must be reasonably forseeable as a consequence of the breach of the duty. The special defenses cover *contributory negligence*, assumption of risk, and *last clear chance*. This is the type of terminology you will be using. Let us see what it means.

The duty of care can arise under the general duty not to injure anyone else, or it can arise under some special *affirmative duty* which is created by the existence of some legal relationship.

Remember the cesspool case we discussed earlier? There, Mrs. Booth was trying to show that Merriam, the landlord, had an affirmative duty to her as a tenant to fix the rotted cesspool cover, and that the breach of that duty caused her injuries. The court, however, ruled that the landlord-tenant relationship did not go that far. But the court did point out that some duty would have existed if Merriam knew of the existence of the defect and Booth did not. At the least, he would have been under an affirmative duty to point out the defect to her.

The concept of breach of duty is easy to grasp. Somebody does something that legally they are not supposed to do. It may be based on affirmative interference with another's property or another's right to act in a certain way; it may be passive refraining from acting toward another when some action is required because of the legal relationship between the parties; or it may include any conduct encompassed by these two extremes.

A police officer without a search warrant illegally enters a house; an automobile driver, without looking behind, backs into a car which is legally parked on the street; a chef in a restaurant fails to refrigerate the cream pies properly and customers get sick; a horse rented from a riding stable throws the rider; a poorly maintained railroad switch sticks and one train runs into another. Each situation entails a breach of some duty of care.

At any given time, there are thousands of lawsuits on file in the courts where negligence is the basis of the action. Most of them concern recognizable everyday duties of care which are taken for granted. Occasionally, an astute lawyer thinks up some new duty that has not been recognized before, and brings a lawsuit based on it. These suits are usually unsuccessful, although once in a while one will stand up to scrutiny. Most of them, however, are far ahead of their time. Judges as a group are extremely conservative and are reluctant to extend the law into new areas of applicability based on the theory enunciated in one lawsuit. After a number of suits raising the issue, and discussion of it in law reviews, this new theory might be followed. Then other states also use it and the new theory becomes an established rule.

When new theories like this arise, they usually hit the newspapers, particularly if they seem outlandish under present-day knowledge and standards. Some recent examples include the man who sued the store that sold a lady a very revealing bathing suit. He claimed he was so distracted watching her that he hit his head going up the ladder to the high-dive board. In another case, a son sued his parents because he did not get a good public school education. His theory was that they acquiesced in his unnecessary absences from high school by giving him false notes to give to the attendance office whenever he asked for them.

I once successfully filed a suit on behalf of a client alleging that the defendant, his neighbor, negligently kept a flock of geese which constantly flew over the client's house

and deposited what are commonly referred to as goose droppings on said plaintiff's driveway, which goose droppings when deposited are in a semi-aqueous state and remain so for several minutes.

The complaint then went on to allege

that the plaintiff, clad only in a bathrobe, went out to get the Sunday paper, stepped on some newly deposited goose droppings, slipped and tore his bathrobe, injuring his hip and exposing his bare body to the taunts and jeers of sundry and various persons then present in the immediate vicinity of said driveway.

This stood up on demurrer, and the court said it had the elements of a valid cause of action.

Like breach of duty, the element of proximate cause is a basic requirement of any tort case. Proximate cause means that the breach of the duty must be connectable through a logical chain of events to the injury suffered by the plaintiff.

Picture an English country fair in the Middle Ages. All the vendors have come early and set up their stalls to display their produce and merchandise to best advantage. One industrious lad has spent the early morning hours making a giant firecracker with a long fuse. By ten o'clock the crowd has assembled. The ale is freely flowing and the firecracker man is glowing. He lights the firecracker and gaily tosses it into the middle of a bunch of vegetables. The excited vegetable man throws it over to the weaver's. The weaver gets rid of it fast and hurls it to the potter. Potter to butcher; butcher to baker; baker to candlestick maker; candlestick maker to draper; draper to picklemonger; picklemonger to—alas, there is no place else to toss it; the fuse has reached the firecracker. It explodes, destroys the stand, and sprays pickles and brine all over the place.

The damaged stall owner sues the original firecracker tosser, who pleads the defense that he did not throw it on the pickle stall, the draper did. The court said that a cause of action arose when the firecracker was first thrown; that the initial toss was the proximate cause in the chain of events which led to the ultimate injury.

When you read this case in law school, the opinion does not mention a firecracker; it talks about a "squib." Some law students who never looked up this word may have not realized that a squib was really a firecracker, and so they never got the full import of the case. I point this out here so that you will be reminded to always look up new terms as soon as you come across them.

Closely connected with proximate cause are the doctrines of forseeability and reasonableness. All through the study of the law, but most particularly in torts, you will be running into "the little man who wasn't there." Nobody has ever seen him. He can be male. He can be female. No one knows what clothes he wears. No one knows what he looks like. But every judge and every lawyer will tell you that he should have been at the scene of every negligent tort that ever occurred. Had he been there, like Superman of Krypton, he would have prevented it from happening. He is the mythical "reasonable man" of the law. The more negligence cases you read, the better you feel you know him. He is the character against whom all actions are tested. Would a reasonable man act the way this plaintiff or that defendant did under exactly the same set of circumstances?

Would a reasonable man foresee the consequences which would result from the defendant's action? The reasonable man concept is one of the big questions in negligence tort cases. Once the jury finds that the defendant's conduct bears a sufficient causal relationship to the plaintiff's injury, they have to determine whether a reasonable man could have foreseen that the harm would have followed from the conduct.

Some years ago, a Supreme Court justice said that he could not give an exact definition of obscenity, but he knew it when he saw it. That is about the status of the reasonable man. Everybody has a sense of who he is and how he thinks, but nobody can describe him with any degree of accuracy. As you study the various cases in torts, however, your concept of the reasonable man will gradually emerge, and eventually, you too will have the feel for his amorphous existence.

Besides testing the defendant's conduct, you will discover that you have to test the plaintiff's as well. Only this time the reasonable man takes the plaintiff's place. The defendant will try to prove that the plaintiff's negligence contributed to the injury. In former days, the finding of the least bit of negligence by the plaintiff would require a defense verdict. This harsh contributory negligence doctrine still exists in many states; however, within the last few years, it is gradually being replaced by the doctrine of comparative negligence. In those jurisdictions following the new rule, the jury is asked to determine the percentage of fault by each party and to apportion the damages between them.

Another defense you will study is "assumption of risk": Knowing the risk, the plaintiff nevertheless went ahead and put himself or herself in the situation which resulted in the injury. A goes to the baseball game and gets hit on the head by a fly ball. Has he assumed a risk inherent in watching the game?

"Last clear chance" is something else you'll run into in tort defenses. If, notwithstanding the plaintiff's contributory negligence, the defendant had the last chance to avoid the injury, judgment may be for the plaintiff.

Besides intentional and negligent torts, the third major class of tort cases you will be exposed to is called *liability without fault*, where the defendant is liable for the injury even if he or she acted with all due care. Here, the liability arises because of the inherently hazardous nature of the activity which the defendant is engaged in—for example, transporting explosives on the highway, experimenting with radioactive materials, or dusting crops with poisonous chemicals.

Another interesting doctrine you will come across in the study of torts is *res ipsa loquitur*, the proof of negligence through circumstantial evidence. Something happens causing an injury. The victim does not know the initial cause. It is the type of thing which is usually the result of negligence. Perhaps the source of knowledge as to its cause is solely within the perspective of the defendant. A is standing on a sidewalk. A flower pot falls from an apartment window ledge and hits her. In a suit against the tenant who put the pot on the sill, res ipsa is used to prove the negligence. The burden is on the defendant to explain what caused the pot to fall.

One reason most students like torts so much is that it is so easy to relate to. We have all been in auto accidents of one kind or another; we have been exposed to all sorts of injuries to our person and property (fortunately without fatal effects, or we would not now be considering a career in law.) As you read each case, and after you know and understand the rule clearly, imagine what you would have done if you were the attorney for one side or the other. Is there any way you could have presented the case to achieve victory for your client?

14

A QUICK LOOK AT FIRST-YEAR COURSES: CRIMES

Law school study of criminal law falls into three categories: substantive, procedural, and constitutional. Substantively, you will be involved in determining what actually is a *crime*; procedurally, in the details of prosecution; constitutionally, in the protections set up for the defendant because the state or federal government is the plaintiff in the lawsuit.

As we noted in the last chapter, practically all intentional torts against individuals or property are crimes in most jurisdictions. Negligence too may be a crime under certain circumstances. Generally, you will be exposed to the idea that, if conduct is grossly without care (reckless), it may be a crime. Most students are unaware, however, that a great deal of all criminal business, in terms of arrest and action taken, is due to negligent conduct by the defendant. Consider for a moment how many traffic tickets have been received because people did not notice a speed limit or a stop sign, or unintentionally violated some other part of a state's Vehicle Code. These and other minor crimes are called *misdemeanors*; the more serious types of crimes are called felonies.

Classically, at common law, crimes were thought of as *malum in se*, those inherently wrong because of their evil nature, and *malum prohibitum*, those prohibited merely because of some statute. Malum in se crimes required the prosecution to prove a specific intent on the part of the defendant to commit the crime. Malum prohibitum only required proof that the defendant knowingly committed the prohibited act. Much of your first year will be spent grasping concepts like this.

You will spend several days studying the difference between *attempts* to commit crimes and actual commission of crimes. For example: A, clearly intending to kill B, hides along a lonely stretch of road one night, rifle in hand, waiting for several hours. Although no one is anywhere in the area, A mistakes a moving tree branch for B and shoots at it. Assuming that these facts could be proven, has A committed attempted murder? Change the facts just a little: C comes walking along and A shoots and kills him, thinking it is B. Change them again: B comes along alone, A points the rifle, but alters his plan and does not shoot. Let us try one more. A points the rifle but just as he shoots at B, a deer runs across the line of sight and is hit by the bullet.

The legal rule that ties these cases together (put into the verbose jargon of the law) is that an attempt is itself a crime if (1) there is a present intent coupled with an apparent or an actual ability to commit a crime; and (2) some overt act is done toward the actual commission of the crime. Generally, the punishment for an attempted crime is less severe than if the crime is actually committed. You might try testing each of the foregoing examples against this rule to see whether you think a conviction for attempted murder would stand up on appeal.

One of the reasons for the wordiness is the desire to be as precise as possible, so that at least those persons having to apply a rule will do so with consistency. Law is far from an exact science, however, and there frequently are opposite verdicts when two persons are charged with the same crime, and even when the same person is tried twice because of some procedural error in the first trial.

A, suspecting he is being set up for the sale of heroin to an undercover narcotics agent, passes ten bundles of a mixture of white flour and milk sugar in exchange for a purchase price agreed upon. Here there is an intent to cheat, not an intent to sell a narcotic substance (even though there was an intent to make a buy), and there is no present ability to consummate the transaction. (No contraband passed between the parties.) The traditional analysis would be that A could not be successfully prosecuted for an attempt to sell heroin. However, he could probably be prosecuted for obtaining money by false pretenses, or larceny by trick and device. Interestingly, because of this legal distinction, many states have passed "turkey laws" making it a narcotics crime to sell imitation narcotics to police agents.

Look for intent-ability questions on law school and bar exams, especially in a question such as, "What crime or crimes, if any, has A committed?" In this type of question, be aware that, if two or more people are engaged in a course of possible criminal conduct, the examiner may want you to discuss the existence of the crimes of *solicitation* (asking someone to commit a crime); *conspiracy* (agreeing with someone to commit a crime—conspiracy to commit a misdemeanor is a felony); *aiding and abetting* (being present and helping in some way but not actually taking part in the crime itself); *accessory before* or *after the fact* (being absent, but participating in the crime by ordering it to occur, advising in its commission, instigating it, or hiding the criminal afterwards); or *compounding a felony* (victim agreeing not to prosecute in exchange for reparation, or accepting a bribe not to testify).

In the substantive law of crimes, you will also be exposed to various crimes and the elements of each. You will find a number of crimes divided into degrees, first degree being the most serious.

The distinction between first- and second-degree murder gives some students trouble. Generally, *first-degree murder* requires (1) a *specific intent* to kill the victim, (2) deliberation (considering in advance whether to perform the deed), and (3) premeditation (making plans to act). Second-degree murder occurs when intent exists but deliberation or premeditation is lacking. Allied with these concepts is the felony murder rule: If during the commission of a felony, someone is killed, even unintentionally, each of the criminals involved can be charged with first- or second-degree murder, depending on the jurisdiction.

A, a burglar, is apprehended in an unlit store. As he is climbing to the roof trying to escape, an officer shoots at him. The bullet kills A's partner B, the lookout. A can be charged with felony-murder.

The next step down from second-degree murder is voluntary manslaughter. The intent to kill exists, deliberation and premeditation are absent, but mitigating circumstances (generally some provocation) exist which make for a lesser crime. If there is no intent to kill, but the defendant acts with extreme recklessness, he or she may be charged with involuntary manslaughter.

In summary:

First-degree Murder: intent, deliberation, and premeditation exist.
Second-degree Murder: intent exists; either deliberation or premeditation absent.
Voluntary Manslaughter: intent exists, but crime occurs during heat of passion.
Involuntary Manslaughter: no intent, but extreme recklessness.

Old courthouse habitués like to tell the story about the friend of a defendant in a famous murder case who bribed a juror to hold out for voluntary manslaughter. After several hours and many ballots, voluntary manslaughter became the verdict. As the juror was being paid off in the back of a nearby bar, he boasted, "This was really a tough one. The rest of the jury kept voting for acquittal, but I finally wore them down."

Aside from homicide, you will also study such crimes as assault, battery, robbery, mayhem, rape, kidnapping, the various types of larceny (theft, embezzlement, false pretense, trick).

Many people are unaware of the difference between *burglary* and *robbery*. Burglary is the entry of a building with the intent to commit some crime; robbery is theft from the person by force or violence. At common law, for burglary to occur there had to be a breaking and entering of a dwelling house in the nighttime. Today, in many jurisdictions, a burglary occurs if there is any entry into any building at any time with the intent to commit some crime. For example, people have been convicted of burglary for going into a department store with the intent to use a fraudulent credit card. Some states make breaking into a locked car to steal something burglary.

You will also learn certain substantive defenses for crimes. You may be surprised to learn that psychiatrists strongly object to the term "insanity" because it is a legal, not a psychiatric, concept. The legal insanity test, based on an old English case, is the "McNaghten Rule," which essentially inquires into the defendant's capacity to determine right from wrong.

A defense which is sometimes argued, but seldom successfully, is intoxication. If it was self-induced, the courts will usually say that a person is responsible for all acts committed while intoxicated. In recent years, however, probably because of strong arguments against the death penalty, courts are permitting a defense of diminished capacity (which may or may not result from intoxication) in murder cases.

An interesting defense is that of infancy: the person is too young to form a criminal intent. The common law conclusively presumed children under 7 years of age incapable of committing any crime, had a rebuttable presumption between 7 and 14, and treated them as adults if they were over 14. A rebuttable presumption is one that exists until facts are shown giving reason for its inapplicability.

The criminal procedure part of the crimes course is closely related to defendants' guaranteed constitutional protections. Criminal procedure is the process of trying and punishing the defendant for the crime. The Warren Court expanded criminal protection in a number of areas, some of which are now being retrenched by a Court composed of different justices. This is compatible with the history of the Supreme Court, where criminal defense protection has periodically expanded and contracted over the last two centuries.

One major contribution to legal analysis engendered by the Warren Court will, however, continue for many years. It had always been the rigid rule that, if something were declared unconstitutional, it was considered to be so from the beginning of the constitutional enactment on which it was based. Accordingly, when the Warren Court determined in *Gideon* v. *Wainright*, 372 U.S. 335 (1963), that it was a violation of due process and equal protection for a state to deny an indigent defendant the services of a lawyer at a felony trial, the Court concluded that it had to follow precedent in applying this new rule. The result was that, in every prior felony case in every state, every defendant who was convicted without the services of a lawyer because he could not afford to hire one to defend him at the trial, was entitled to a retrial regardless of how long ago the trial had been held. Because of the staleness of the evidence, absence of witnesses, and inability of local district attorneys to handle the increased case loads, few of these retrials could take place. Thousands of hard-core criminals then in state prisons had to be released.

The public outcry was tremendous. And when the Court started defining other constitutional protections—such as prohibition of use of confessions made at time of arrest without warning against self-incrimination, right to a lawyer before having to answer any questions by the police, and the state duty to provide a lawyer for an indigent arrestee if one was requested—the clamor from the citizenry and law enforcement grew louder and louder. The Court stood fast, however, and retrials were ordered throughout the land. Evidence previously believed valid was found inadmissible, and again, numerous convicts who had confessed to their crimes were set free.

Gradually, without much public awareness even to this day, the Court started to erode the doctrine of *retroactivity*. By the time Chief Justice Warren retired, a new rule was established that a decision could be nonretroactive if the Court said so. It would not be applied to activities occurring before that time.

We now find some decisions even being made prospectively; the Court will sometimes give a new interpretation of the law which is not applied even to the case being decided but is set down to regulate future conduct. While this may make unnecessary the sudden release of large numbers of convicts, it has another effect which in the long run may be more dangerous. Prospective decision making is essentially judicial legislation. Five justices can now tell the entire country what the law will have to be in the future, thus clouding Congress's power to enact statutes which, under the former rule, would have been enacted before being passed upon by the Court. By proclaiming a rule to operate in the future, the Court is in effect telling Congress in advance not to enact a certain statute. Prospective decision making has also been picked up by several state supreme courts, and state legislatures are now coming under subtle restraint from judicial legislation.

Today, in every state, felony crimes are prosecuted either by *indictment* by a grand jury or an information filed by the prosecuting attorney. In the federal system, the Constitution requires an indictment.

Under the indictment system, outside the presence of the prospective defendant, the prosecutor presents only the government side of the case to the grand jury. (Some jurisdictions allow a prospective defendant to testify, too.) If they believe a crime has been committed, they issue an indictment accusing some one. This becomes the complaint in the criminal trial.

In the information method, some person files a *complaint* accusing an individual of committing a crime; a *preliminary hearing* is set before a magistrate; the prosecution has to put on enough evidence to show reasonable cause to believe that the defendant has committed the crime; the defendant can cross-examine witnesses and put on evidence if desired; the magistrate determines whether the defendant should be held to answer to the county court. If so, the prosecutor issues an information accusing the defendant of the crime. This then becomes the complaint in the criminal trial. Several years ago, the United States Supreme Court decided that a preliminary hearing was also required in indictment cases, before the defendant could be brought to trial.

Before trial, the defendant is given an opportunity to enter a plea to the charge. The customary pleas are Not Guilty, Not Guilty by Reason of Insanity, Guilty, or *Nolo Contendere* (no contest). For all practical purposes, the *Nolo* plea is similar to a Guilty plea. The difference is that the former may not be used to find liability in a civil case. A plea of Guilty, or a finding of guilty on trial, may be used in a civil case in some states.

A is convicted of manslaughter in the drunk driving death of B. B's widow brings a civil wrongful death action for damages against A. The judgment of conviction in the criminal trial can be admitted in evidence in the civil case as proof that A was drunk when he was driving the car that hit B, and that the impact was the proximate cause of B's death. This use of the criminal conviction considerably cuts down on the time necessary to try the civil case and allows the parties to get down to deciding how much the damages should be.

All criminal defendants in felony cases are entitled to a jury trial. They are entitled to a lawyer at all stages of the proceedings; if they cannot afford one, the state must provide one at no cost. After arrest, and during trial, the defendant is entitled to be released on bail. The purpose of bail is to insure the defendant's presence during subsequent proceedings.

If the verdict is Not Guilty, the defendant is free. If it is Guilty, a probation and sentence report is ordered. Based upon this report and sometimes on other information, the defendant is put on probation or incarcerated for the term prescribed by law. A defendant may be paroled prior to expiration of sentence. Violation of parole may result in reincarceration. When the sentence time ends, the individual is freed.

A defendant who is found guilty is entitled to appeal. Again, in felony cases, a lawyer is provided free if the defendant cannot afford to pay for the services. Normally, the prosecution may not appeal after a Not Guilty verdict.

Experience has shown that most career, paid, public defenders do an excellent job at both trial and appellate levels. Many people have the idea that these individuals are hack lawyers. That is not the case. Public defenders are specialists. All they do is try criminal cases. They have access to investigative sources a private paying client might not be able to afford. They have a daily working relationship with the judges. They go up against the same group of lawyers from the D.A.'s office all the time, are aware of the trial tactics these prosecutors personally use to sway juries, and know how to combat them. They know the ins and outs of plea bargaining. They know all the details of alternative sentencing. They know how to get the best possible deal for their clients. Most important, they are dedicated.

As you study crimes, you will get the deep feeling that our Constitution is a truly wonderful document and that the rights it provides all persons are simply spectacular. In your career as a law student and a lawyer you will get a new concept of the right of an individual not to be required to testify against himself or herself; the right to equal protection of the law; the right to be free from unreasonable or warrantless searches and seizures; the right to due process; the right to trial by jury, and all the other rights set forth.

You will gradually come to understand that, while it may sometimes seem bad for society to give criminals so many rights, it would be worse if those rights did not exist for anyone. Consider that every right which may be enforced to benefit some terrible criminal is also enforced to protect some innocent citizen when he or she gets into trouble for perhaps the first time. The existence of these constitutional rights is the protection we all have against the excessive use of power by agents of any governing body in the country.

15

A QUICK LOOK AT FIRST-YEAR COURSES: PROPERTY

Property is probably the most complicated first-year course. The concepts and subject matter are relatively foreign to most people's experience.

The *personal property* part is fairly easy to relate to because it is familiar. Questions will be raised as to who owns the expensive ring that is found in the back of an old safe purchased from the Salvation Army. Can the owner of stolen property get it back from someone who bought it in good faith from the thief? Is the restaurant responsible to the diner if someone walks off with a coat? You will learn about property called *fixtures* that may be real or personal, depending on the circumstances. Do the window shades go with the building? How about the large fruit trees in big, oaken half-barrels that border the patio? What about the two-ton statue of Aphrodite's grandmother sitting in the middle of the front lawn?

Is there such a thing as squatters rights? Does a property owner have to file a law suit to protect rights to the property? What happens when someone purchases a piece of land described in complicated surveyor's language in the deed and the survey is incorrect? There is one case where the surveyor got turned around 180 degrees and came back on the same line.

Suppose you build your house on the wrong lot?

Who owns the land from the curb to the middle of the street?

When you buy land by the acre and there is a very high hill on the property, do you measure the acreage as you go up the side of the hill—which results in less actual land—or do you measure the acre along a flat plane, as if the hill didn't exist—in which case you get more?

Much of *real property* law comes from the old English ways of holding land. Full outright ownership was known as "*fee simple* absolute." If the land had to stay in the family blood line it was called "fee tail." "Fee tail male" or "fee tail female" meant it could only pass to male or female blood relatives.

There is a whole area of study concerning the rights of tenants, rights between tenants, length of tenancy, and so on.

Another subject division called *easements* covers the right to use someone else's property for a specific purpose. A flood control district purchases an easement to divert flood waters over certain farm lands during the rainy season. Does this give the district the right to permit the public to use the temporary body of water for hunting and fishing? Or can the farmers consider the public trespassers and put them off the property?

A good way to get into real property problems is to go to the law library before the semester starts and read some historical background material. There are some old works by Pollack and Maitland covering the feudal period which you will find very worthwhile. A few hours browsing through Blackstone's *Commentaries* could also prove educational and enjoyable.

You will be exposed to the concepts of limitations, *future interests* and *estates*. What kind of restrictions can be put on the future use of property? Land is donated to a school district for use as long as an elementary school is maintained on the premises. Fifty years later, the neighborhood has changed and only a few old people still live there. If the school is closed and the property put up for sale, do the heirs of the original grantor have any right to claim that the land should go back to them?

Bible Belt property is originally sold only to members of a certain religious sect, with the intent that they will build houses there and live as a tightly knit community. The deed restrictions bar resale or transfer to persons not following the tenets of the faith. One couple dies, leaving no heirs except an atheist niece in Chicago. Can she move into the house? Can she sell it?

In general, you will come to realize that when lawyers refer to property, it is not so much the physical object as the right of an individual to hold and control it, dispose of it, or prevent others from using it. You will learn that within the concept of total ownership, there are still restrictions which have been set by historical precedent and statutory enactment. For example, an owner cannot dig a hole so close to the property line that lateral structural support is taken away, causing a neighbor's building to fall. Another limitation on owners' rights is a doctrine known as the Rule Against Perpetuities. This old common law doctrine, still current in some variation in a number of states, prevents disposition of an estate to an unborn individual not conceived within the life time of persons named by a testator in a will, plus 21 years.

Suppose a woman with one son, and no other living heirs, wanted to tie up her real property and will it to her great-grandchildren. If at the time of her death, and thereafter, the son had no children, there would never be any great-grandchild to inherit the estate. At the end of the 21-year period, or on his earlier death without children, the estate would be divided as if this special provision were not in the will. If there were no contingency provision, she would be considered *intestate* (having no will) as to the portion set aside for great-grandchildren.

On the other hand, if the son had a living child at, or after, the mother's death, and that child (her grandchild) also had a child conceived within the 21-year period, then there would be a great-grandchild eligible to inherit.

When someone dies intestate (leaving no valid will) as to all or part of an estate, the court distributes the unwilled property according to certain formal rules established by the common law, or as changed by statute. Generally, the purpose is to locate the nearest living relative. Occasionally, this leads to the "laughing heir" situation—the person who one day answers a knock at the door and learns that some unknown cousin of her great-grandfather had died in Australia, and she is now the sole owner of a sheep ranch.

16

SOME OBSERVATIONS ON CONSTITUTIONAL LAW

Of all the courses you will study in law school, constitutional law will probably be the most exciting, since the Constitution is the ultimate law of the country. The way it is interpreted can mean the allowance or prohibition of any federal, state, or local governmental activity. Generally speaking, that's what the study of constitutional law is all about. Some governmental activity is challenged, and the Supreme Court tells us whether it is valid or not.

Things which have continued for years without change suddenly are altered because some lawyer seemingly has convinced the Court to accept a new theory or declare a new rule. Most of the time, however, research will show that the ideas behind it have been around for a long time, and attempts to put them across have been orchestrated before this and other courts for years.

So you will be aware of how the Supreme Court rulings get down to the lower courts, keep the following in mind:

There are fifty-one major legal jurisdictions in the United States: fifty states and the federal government. Each has its own set of laws and its own rules of procedure. All state and federal courts are bound by the federal Constitution and the decisions of the United States Supreme Court. State courts are bound by their state constitutions, and by the decisions of their highest state court. If a state wants to, it can give all persons within its borders greater protection than the federal Constitution requires. The federal *district courts* are bound by the rulings of the United States Circuit Court of Appeals for the circuit in which they are located. On a federal constitutional question, a federal district court can, in a proper case, overrule the highest court of a state.

Many people erroneously believe that the entire first ten amendments, constituting the Bill of Rights of the federal Constitution, are automatically applicable to the states. They are only applicable to the federal government, except for those specific words which have been made applicable to the states by Supreme Court decisions. There is, however, an ongoing legal controversy over whether or not a sentence in Section 1 of the Fourteenth Amendment can be used to make the entire Bill of Rights applicable to state activities:

No State shall make or enforce any laws which shall abridge the privileges or immunities of citizens of the United States; nor shall any State deprive any person of life, liberty or property, without due process of law; nor deny to any person within its jurisdiction the equal protection of the laws.

The Supreme Court has never accepted this argument. While some of the justices have occasionally indicated a belief in that direction, collectively they have been extremely cautious in spreading the blanket, preferring to expand the constitutional protections on a case-by-case basis.

How do new ideas get generated in the first place? As an example, let us look at Article I, section 8, subdivision 1, of the Constitution:

The Congress shall have the power to lay and collect taxes, duties, imposts and excises, to pay the debts and provide for the common defense and general welfare of the United States; but all duties, imposts and excises shall be uniform throughout the United States. . . .

The thinking lawyer will read this and perhaps observe that, while Congress is given the "power to lay and collect taxes, duties, imposts and excises" (four items), only "duties, imposts and excises [three items] shall be uniform throughout the United States." Could the exclusion from the uniformity clause possibly mean that the imposition and collection of federal taxes may be done on a non-uniform basis throughout the country? Does this give Congress the power to pass legislation taxing New Yorkers differently from Oregonians?

Does such a theory conflict in any way with Article I, section 9, subdivision 4:

No capitation, or other direct, tax shall be laid, unless in proportion to the census or enumeration hereinbefore directed to be taken.

What about Article IV, section 2, subdivision 1:

The citizens of each State shall be entitled to all privileges and immunities of citizens in the several States.

Does the Sixteenth Amendment affect the validity of this theory:

The Congress shall have the power to lay and collect taxes on incomes, from whatever source derived, without apportionment among the several States, and without regard to any census or enumeration.

This discussion is an illustration of just one way that novel legal ideas may happen to be created. Normally, lawyers don't just sit around and say, "What can I come up with today that will make legal history?" Theories are developed in trying to work out possible solutions to actual problems.

When I successfully represented the State of California and argued *Richardson* v. *Ramirez*, 418 U.S. 24, 94 S. Ct. 2655, 41 L.Ed. 2d 551 (1974) in the United States Supreme Court, I was advocating the validity of a California Constitution provision which denied the right to vote to any person who had been convicted of a felony. The State Supreme Court had several years previously ruled that this provision applied only to a felony which had some connection with the elective process, and left the determination of that question to each county clerk.

SLAYING THE LAW SCHOOL DRAGON

As a result of many different interpretations, persons who had completed their sentences were allowed to vote in one country but not in another. Thus, in Los Angeles County, a conviction of rape did not disenfranchise; but in the same county, statutory rape did, on the theory that seducing a minor involved some element of fraud or trickery which carried over to the possibility of corruption in the casting or counting of votes. The same county prohibited a check forger or embezzler from voting, but let a bank robber do so. In another county, there would be a different result, depending on the whim or bias of the county clerk as to the nature of the particular crime. There was an obvious denial of equal protection by the state to convicted felons who had finished their terms and desired to vote.

The appellant claimed that the California Constitution provision violated that part of Fourteenth Amendment, Section 1, which reads:

No State shall make or enforce any law which shall abridge the privileges or immunities of citizens of the United States; nor shall any State . . . deny to any person within its jurisdiction the equal protection of the laws.

Research indicated that some old Supreme Court cases gave an inference that the Fourteenth Amendment, Section 2, might apply by analogy. Ostensibly, it dealt with the number of representatives a State would be given in Congress, based on the population, but reduced the count if certain persons were disenfranchised. It provides:

Representatives shall be apportioned among the several States according to their respective numbers, counting the whole number of persons in each State, excluding Indians not taxed. But *when the right to vote at any election* for the choice of electors for President and Vice President of the United States, Representatives in Congress, the executive and judicial officers of a State, or the members of the Legislature thereof, *is denied to any of the male inhabitants of such State, being twenty-one years of age, and citizens of the United States, or in any way abridged, except for participation in rebellion or other crime*, the basis of representation therein shall be reduced in the proportion which the number of such male citizens shall bear to the whole number of male citizens twenty-one years of age in such State.

The Court accepted my argument that under this section, state denial of equal protection in voting was not prohibited, merely penalized, and not even that in the case of rebels or criminals: it took the Fifteenth Amendment to let blacks vote; the Nineteenth Amendment to let women vote; the Twenty-sixth Amendment to let minors vote; and it will take another amendment to let felons vote.

So you will have the whole story, after this case the California Constitution was amended to delete the prohibition against voting by felons.

As you go through your courses, you will realize that new concepts sometimes arise in areas which have for years been considered solid and unchangeable, because some lawyer interpreted the old language in a new way. But, as in this instance, there usually has been some prior discussion foreshadowing the change.

Generally, outside of some passing reference in your constitutional law course, there will be very little stress on the techniques used to interpret statutory language. One important thing to do is to get copies of each of the variations in a bill, from the time it was first introduced by a legislator, through all the amendments until final passage.

There are numerous rules of statutory interpretation, all laid out in the legal treatises and encyclopedias found in any good law library. They have been developed over the years by the courts and are often used to rationalize a desired position. Years ago, a learned judge wrote an article describing the process of judicial thinking in the development of new law. He concluded that the opinion writer first gets an unrealized subconscious bias which permeates his analysis and energizes his research in some particular direction; then he reaches his conclusion and goes looking for law to back up his position, creating new rules if necessary by stretching old ones almost beyond recognition, but always leaving them identifiable to satisfy compliance with the doctrine of *stare decisis*: to stand by decisions and not to disturb matters which have been settled.

17

HOW TO STUDY FOR EXAMS

If you have studied your cases for the daily lecture far enough in advance, taken down what the professor has said in class, and done as much outside reading as possible in texts, outlines, and law review articles, you will probably get fairly good grades on your exams.

The most important thing in studying for exams is organization. First, plan your time so you can start studying for finals at least three weeks before the test date. This is especially important. And you should be completely finished at least two nights before an exam is given. If you wind up cramming the night before an exam, you will take the test under great stress and it will be a lot tougher to come up with good answers. You may not believe this advice works; but if you feel it is necessary to look over your notes the night before an exam, at least be sure you have finished studying, so that all you do is look over. Do not leave any learning until the last minute. Procrastination is the Lorelei of the legal profession. If you succumb to her siren song, you will be dashed against the rocks.

The first thing to do is go over the casebook table of contents, which you have already memorized. This should immediately bring all the major points back to you. Then go through each case in your casebook, studying the rule you wrote at the top before the semester started; use the mnemonic stick figure to bring back the facts of the case, and carefully read marginal notes which you may have added during class discussions, memorizing any summation lists the professor may have given out. If something is not clear, read the case itself for clarification. Supplement your studying with any other outlines or summation material you have.

Frequently, in your studies, you will find that the general rule for some proposition is divided into a majority and a minority view. Each of these divergent views may in turn depend on the resolution of the facts which the trier has reached in a given situation. You should be able to set these variations up into something resembling a geneology table or a decision tree. The kind of material exam question designers are drawn to lends itself readily to this approach.

The question will inevitably arise: Should you study alone or with others? After many years of helping friends get through law school and pass the bar exam, I'm convinced that the *first* study and review should be alone. This applies to daily class work as well as exams.

Communal study is often very profitable, but it's better to study by yourself until you are sure you know the material. Only then, go through a workout with others. There may be a couple of points you have overlooked or misunderstood. But in the main, you will find yourself ahead of your colleagues. Because of your superior knowledge resulting from the way you have prepared, you will find yourself teaching and explaining to them. This will greatly reinforce your own learning. It will also send you into the exam with the confidence you need to do your best in the most relaxed manner.

After any joint discussion sessions, leave yourself enough time to do your own final review. You may discover that you have picked up some wrong approaches which need correction.

I do not want to leave you with the impression that you should be a loner. One of the most valuable aspects of law school is the constant, informal give and take among students, where hairs are split and the growing knowledge of the law being acquired is applied to all kinds of imagined situations designed to test the rules being learned.

Most students do not realize that in writing a question, the examiner often tries to guide the student into the specific area of the law on which discussion is expected. For example, there is a doctrine in contracts called the *Statute of Frauds*. It really has little to do with fraud. It concerns the requirement that certain types of contracts must be in writing or they will not be enforced by the courts—such as a contract for the sale of real property. Like all major doctrines, this one contains exceptions. It is the study of these doctrines or rules, and the exceptions to them, which comprise much of the study of the law. Thus, if an exam question in contracts gives a lot of facts, and incidentally says the agreement between the parties is in writing, this may be a signal the professor wants you to recognize that the Statute of Frauds issue is not applicable, and then go on to discuss the other issues raised.

At the start of any particular course, you will not have much feel for what it is all about, only a general idea of where you are headed based on your preliminary preparation. Later on, as your knowledge deepens, various parts of the course will fall into logical sequence. It will be extremely helpful when taking exams if you have developed a system to help you summarize each section. A good way to do this is to make up your own hypothetical set of facts to cover a particular subsection of the course. Let us look at the area known as *quasi-contracts*, sometimes part of a course called Remedies or Restitution. For the first several weeks, the incantations sound something like this: "unjust enrichment," "reasonable value of the benefit received," "contract implied in fact," "contract implied in law."

Start with Harvey Brown of Middlebore, Anystate, U.S.A. He lives in a tract house across the river in the Blissville area. Every house is exactly the same for a mile in each direction. One day, Harvey is at the Middlebore Service Club weekly luncheon, sitting next to Joe, the roofer.

"Joe, old Service Club buddy, how much will you charge me to roof that little place of mine over on Wishing Well Lane in the Blissville area?"

"For you, Harv," says Joe, after thinking a minute and making a quick calculation on the tablecloth, "fifty-four hundred dollars."

"That sounds pretty good, Joe. When can your guys get over to do the job?"

"How's next Thursday? Okay?"

"Okay."

This is an actual contract, even though not in writing. It is called a contract implied in fact. Harvey has legally contracted to pay Joe the fifty-four hundred dollars when he has finished the job. They polish off the mashed potatoes and broccoli, listen to the guest speaker, and then take off to their offices.

Next Thursday arrives. Joe's men are going over to Harvey's on the roofing truck. By mistake, they miss Harvey's house and hit one just like it on the next street. They put the ladder up against the wrong house, the Machiavellis'. Mrs. Machiavelli, hanging out the wash, watches what is going on and thinks, "If I keep quiet, we'll get a free roof job."

Although Joe's people made a mistake, it would be unconscionable to allow Mrs. Machiavelli to profit by the error which she knew of but did nothing to prevent. After all, she received the benefit of the roof job. The law will not permit her to be unjustly enriched. It will imply a contract in law to rectify the situation. That means that although the parties (Joe and Mrs. Machiavelli) did not actually have a contract, the law will treat them as if they did. "Quasi-contract" means "like a contract" and is the remedy used to put people whole again (where they would have been if nothing had happened), even if there is no actual contract, when one individual is unjustly enriched at the expense of another.

If Joe's men had put the roof on Harvey's house in accordance with the terms of the original contract, and Harvey did not pay, Joe could sue Harvey for the contract price, $5,400. But what is the measure of damages (how much can Joe get) in the quasi-contract suit if he has to take Mrs. Machiavelli to court? The law says it is the reasonable value of the benefit received. Here, the roof job may be worth more or less than $5,400. Joe may have given Harvey a special price. That amount is only some evidence of what a reasonable value might be. At a trial, Joe would testify and would also bring in expert witnesses from the roofing business to state their opinions as to reasonable value. The amount determined by the trier of fact (jury or judge, as the case might be) would be the amount of recovery (what Joe gets if he wins).

Suppose that instead of being home hanging clothes out on the line, Mrs. Machiavelli was away on vacation. Since she did not compound the error, because she did not have knowledge of it, she would not have been unjustly enriched. She would get a free roof job whether she needed one or not.

Through this hypothetical example, the quasi-contracts segment of the remedies course is now neatly packaged for subsequent use, and it is easy to resurrect the principle: Quasi-contract is the remedy for unjust enrichment, damages being awarded for the reasonable value of the benefit received.

Without realizing it, you will gradually find that you are starting to talk like a lawyer. And once you get an area of the law categorized like this one, so you can use it when an analogous situation arises, you will start thinking like a lawyer, too.

During my first year of law practice I had an interesting experience with quasi-contracts. To help with expenses, and also to get known around town as a lawyer, I had been teaching a law-for-laypersons course at the local adult evening school. One of my students dropped in with a case. He had worked about ten years for the biggest bank in the community and was chagrined because he did not win a hoped-for promotion.

As part of his duties, he had been the bank notary public. The company had paid for his seal, application fee, and official bond premium. It required him to charge notary fees to small depositors and noncustomers of the bank, but made him do the work free for the bank itself and its big customers. All fees received were placed in a special account in his name. At the end of each month, the accumulated balance was transferred to the company employees' recreational welfare fund. Huffed at being overlooked for promotion, he had quit his job and now wanted to sue the bank for the notary fees.

Notaries are appointed by the governor in most states and are considered to be independent public officials. The law in most states is that the fees an official receives in the performance of his or her duties are sacrosanct; they belong to the official, and it is improper to refuse to pay them or take them away. I had mentioned this in class in an offhand way one night, not realizing the special value it would have for this student.

On his behalf, I wrote a letter to the branch manager of the bank, saying something like, "When Joe Blow left your employ yesterday, you inadvertently forgot to pay him for the notary fees which he collected in his official capacity, and which we have computed to be $1,100. Undoubtedly, you will wish to correct this oversight promptly. You may do so by sending your check to him, care of the undersigned. If we do not hear from you within ten days, appropriate legal action will be instituted to collect this sum."

(Be extremely careful about what you say when you write a letter to someone requesting payment of a debt to a client. Never imply that criminal action will be taken if payment is not forthcoming. This is a particularly easy trap to fall into if someone has, for example, given your client a bad check. The threat to go to the D.A. and file a complaint charging the debtor with prosecution for forgery or insufficient funds constitutes extortion, a felony. Occasionally, overzealous young lawyers write dunning letters that go over this line, and once in awhile they get prosecuted by a D.A. and disciplined by their state supreme court.)

The bank manager called my office about four times the next morning while I was in court. He wanted to come over to my office right away. Although we had met previously at a few local functions, he had never been too friendly before. Now he was all frozen smiles and oil. He even called me "Mister" when he shook my hand.

Getting right down to business, he told me how I was new in town and what a great future I had ahead of me; too bad I was jeopardizing it by representing someone like his former employee. After all, trying to get the bank's money like this was tantamount to trying to steal it. The bank had paid all the expenses; what did this employee mean by making such an outlandish claim? In all the years he had been a bank manager, he had never heard of such a thing.

By this time, his harangue was getting pretty thick, so I shoved one of the California Supreme Court Reports across the desk at him and asked him if he had ever heard of the case on page 198. I then leaned over, picked up the book and read him something like this from the decision I was referring to: "The Notary Public is the long arm of the Governor in the provinces. It is an offense against the sovereign to refuse to pay or to take from that official his legally authorized fees. Under such circumstances, there is an unjust enrichment for which the Notary Public may bring an action in quasi-contract against the wrongdoer."

The bank manager quickly changed the subject back to what a great future there was for me; he told me how much business the bank could send me and said they would be doing a great service to their customers by the referrals, because evidently I was a pretty smart lawyer. Then he maneuvered into the suggestion that it would be the best thing for everyone concerned if he recommended to his committee that they settle this case for $100—not because of the bank's liability, of course, but just for the nuisance value involved in the claim.

Although I was annoyed by the implied bribe attempt, I tried not to show it, and shook his hand as we got up toward the door. Then I said, "That will be great. You make that recommendation to your committee. But tell them I never agreed to it and that it's solely your idea. And while you are telling them that, also tell them if I don't have a check for the full amount of eleven hundred dollars by noon tomorrow, I'll file suit against the bank for every document he ever notarized for them free within the period of the statute of limitations; and perhaps I'll even file a class action against the bank on behalf of all the other notaries in the other branches."

That afternoon, the senior partner of the leading law firm in town called to see what he could do the ameliorate the matter. I told him what happened and cited the case on page 198 of the Supreme Court Reports. He said that he would study it and get back to me.

At eleven-thirty the next morning a bank messenger appeared at my office with a check for $1,100, payable to my client, and a release form for my client to sign, agreeing that any claim he had against the bank had been settled.

Some weeks later, I learned that this particular banking chain had issued an order to all branches that same afternoon, discontinuing the use of any notaries who worked for the bank, even for the bank's own documents.

18

HOW TO ANSWER
EXAM QUESTIONS

A good answer to any essay exam question will usually include identification of the basic issues or doctrines in the question, a statement of the relevant rules and exceptions, the application of these rules to the facts presented, and a conclusion which logically follows. Law school questions generally will be confined to the scope of the course. Essay questions on the bar exam, however, will often mix more than one subject. In law school, the emphasis is on course content. While this is vital in bar exam questions, the examiners are also greatly interested in whether you can think like a lawyer.

There is a growing tendency on bar exams to have fewer essay questions and more computer-correctable, true–false and multiple-choice items. The principles of analysis, however, remain the same. The examiners are still trying to determine whether you should be released to the world and allowed to handle client problems within the framework of the legal system. How well can you utilize what you have learned to best protect your client's interest in any given situation?

A good lawyer looks at every problem from all possible perspectives. Remember that every legal problem has adversary connotations. This is easy to see when you are in the middle of a lawsuit, but it is also true, for example, when you are drafting a statute or giving advice on a course of action to follow in future business conduct.

So, when you take any law exam, keep in mind that you are in training to be a lawyer. When I studied for the bar, I took a quiz course given by three people. One taught *substantive law*—contracts, torts, corporations. A second taught adjective law—practice, procedure, evidence. The third taught how to pass the bar exam.

To this day, I can see that last man, a natural comedian, standing on the stage smoking a cigar. He said, "They throw an old lady in your office; she's got three kids—one has polio, another has pneumonia, and the third just flunked her rabbit test; it's snowing outside; the mortgage is due. . . ." Then he threw the cigar on the floor, jumped on it, and yelled, "The answer is NO!" His message was clear. On the bar, do not get sucked into a vortex of sympathy so you cannot solve the problem presented. This does not mean that the answer could not be "yes." It is just a caution to beware writing like a sympathetic social worker instead of a lawyer.

The "no" approach is good one to use on essay exams for those parts of questions where "yes" might seem to suggest itself.

Here is a sample bar exam question, so you can see how the "no" method (where you take a negative approach) works. This particular question concerns both torts and wills.

Mrs. Jones, a woman of exemplary character, appears in your office in a common law jurisdiction and informs you that her husband has just died and his will is about to be probated. In it, he has called her a common prostitute and has left her only a dollar. Discuss her rights and remedies.

A good answer might run something like this:

The common law of torts is divided into three general areas: intentional or malicious conduct, negligent conduct, and liability without fault due to the extra-hazardous nature of the activity.

Here, in writing his will, a husband has accused his wife, a woman of exemplary character, of being a common prostitute. This is defamation of character, a malicious tort. Since it is in writing, it is libel; were it oral, it would be slander.

No action will lie at common law, however, for two reasons: (1) A

118

husband could not commit a tort against his wife; and (2) all tort actions died with the death of the perpetrator of the tort, the *tort-feasor*.

No action will lie against the lawyer who drew the will because any information he received from his client, the husband, was subject to the lawyer-client privilege. This privilege extends to the lawyer's secretary who typed the will as she is considered an arm of the lawyer.

No action will lie against the executor who filed the will for probate, as his act is also privileged because he was under a legal duty to make such a filing.

No action will lie against the court or any of its officials because of the privilege afforded to judicial actions.

No action will lie against the estate of the husband because, as previously stated, the tort remedy, if any existed, died with the death of the tort feasor.

As you can see, as of this point in our analysis, the "no" approach has enabled us to give a broad discussion of the applicable law of torts, setting forth principles and exceptions. To wrap up the answer to the question, let us look at the wills part for a moment.

While there can be no recovery under the law of torts, there are several areas under the law of wills which may afford the wife relief.

Under the majority rule, where a husband is so mistaken as to his wife's true nature that he erroneously considers her to be a common prostitute, when she is a woman of exemplary character, such a statement in a will is conclusive evidence that the husband lacked the required testamentary capacity to make the will. He was not of "sound mind" at the time the will was executed. The widow should be successful in moving to set aside the will and keep it from being admitted to probate.

Since the husband did not leave a valid will when he died, he is said to have died intestate. The widow may apply for appointment as administratrix of the estate. During the pendency of the administration she is entitled to a widow's allowance. She is entitled to receive administratrix's fees. She is entitled to be awarded dower rights on distribution of the estate.

If you take the bar exam in a community property state, throw in a possible extra-credit line or two to the effect that if this had taken place in a community property state, the husband had a right to will away only half of the community assets in any event, and the other half would have automatically passed to the wife outside of probate.

Notice that I did not give a case citation of any kind. Examiners do not expect you to be a walking research library, and if you give a wrong citation, some may mark you down.

Commercially prepared study outlines are useful to supplement whatever materials you have prepared for yourself. Many of these have detailed methods of problem analysis which will be of immense help on school exams; for the bar, when they are given out as supplements to a good bar review course, they are a must.

Also take a look at some of the exam "quizzers" in your legal bookstore which have sample bar questions and answers broken down by course subject. These will give you some model answers to routine problems, variations of which often come up on final law school exams.

19

HOW TO WRITE A BRIEF

A brief is a formal, written argument, usually presented to an appellate court, for the purpose of convincing the justices hearing the case to rule in favor of the side on whose behalf it is presented. The brief should discuss each issue under contention, persuasively set forth the law applicable to the facts of the case, and point out any flaws in the opponent's position. Because the basis of every decision is the analysis of the legal points set forth by each side in the briefs presented to the court, it is very helpful to be familiar with how briefs are constructed and what they contain.

Most law schools have an activity called Moot Court in which first year students are encouraged to participate. Moot Court is a make-believe appellate court. It is a good experience and gets you involved in legal research fairly rapidly. Usually, you are given a reasonable period of time to do your preparation. But start as soon as possible. It takes a lot of effort, and if you put it off, you will do a poor job.

A hypothetical statement of facts containing one or more novel legal issues not yet decided by real courts is presented to the participating students. Working from that perspective, they have to prepare and submit briefs, and then argue the case before a simulated judicial tribunal. (In actual practice, you get a reporter's transcript of the trial and have to dig out the facts yourself.) The same principles apply to both Moot Court and actual briefs.

Although only a small percentage of all cases tried are actually appealed, cases won at trial are occasionally lost before a reviewing court. As you read the cases in your casebook, watch for these instances and see if you could have foreseen the possibility of error if you had tried the case in the court below.

P's and A's is lawyer jargon for *points and authorities*. They are like little briefs, and are customarily presented to trial judges to cover principles applicable to specific legal questions which may arise during the course of the litigation.

Most lawyers in private practice get very little chance to go into the appellate courts, and many are apprehensive at the idea of writing a brief. Many go for years without doing so. Thus do everything you can while you are a student to gain brief-writing experience. It will pay off in a number of ways. Most important, writing briefs expands your law-finding ability. As you do your research and think about various arguments you may wish to use, you begin to see that there are numerous ways to approach a problem.

You will discover that the indices to legal literature are only as helpful as the acumen of the persons who prepared them. Cases sometimes do not hold what headnotes indicate. You may occasionally find that when you look up a topic in an index, it will refer you to some other word or phrase; then, when you look at the second place, you are referred back to the first. Other times, you think something is very elementary, but you just cannot find anything listed on the subject. After a short time, however, familiarity with the indices pays off in rapid progress in research. As you gain more experience and knowledge of the law, you will develop more ideas on where to look. Analogous legal doctrines will suggest themselves, and frequently, persuasive new arguments will come to the fore.

Competency in legal research, besides expanding your ability to determine what current law is, will enable you to find faster, more effective answers to your clients' problems. And when you are pressed for time in a trial, you will be able to give the judge a quick applicable citation to tide you over until you have time to prepare P's and A's.

The physical style of brief writing has become fairly formalized. Practically all appellate courts have detailed rules as to size of pages, type specifications, arrangement of contents, number of copies, and so on. Check the rules for the jurisdiction you are in (in law school, its the Moot Court Rules) to make sure the clerk will accept your papers when you are ready to file them. Incidentally, be very careful of time deadlines or you may find your appeal is dismissed.

Courts generally require printed briefs. Some will also accept good quality typed reproductions. There are specific rules as to what color the cover of each of the parties' briefs must be. This is to help the justices so they know what brief they will be reading when they pick it up.

Generally, brief formats are similar; but jurisdictional requirements vary. The brief starts out with a title page which gives the name of the appellate court; the name of the case; the title, such as "Appellant's Reply Brief"; the name of the court where the action arose; and the name, address and telephone number of the lawyer filing the brief. After the title page comes the Table of Contents (sometimes called the Subject Index). As in any book, it is usually an index to the material by section headings. It is a good practice to copy the full text of the section headings into the Table of Contents so the reader will have an overview picture of your entire argument. If there is an intermediate court opinion, that usually comes next. Then comes a page stating the major issues to be covered in the brief. These are referred to as "Questions Presented." All briefs have one; some contain more. In writing the question, most brief writers try to get everything into one sentence. Sometimes this gets ridiculously long and cumbersome. Do not be afraid to split one question into two for clarity. Try to put something special into this section which will make the court want to read what you have to say. A brief is a selling document. Each word should be carefully chosen for its effect on the justices who you hope will buy your side of the argument.

In *Richardson* v. *Ramirez*, which I mentioned in Chapter 16, this is what the questions section of the brief looked like:

QUESTIONS PRESENTED

Can a state constitutionally disenfranchise convicted felons who are otherwise qualified to vote?

a. Does the denial of voting rights for "participation in rebellion, or other crime" language of the United States Constitution, Amendment XIV, Section 2, override the "equal protection" clause of Amendment XIV, Section 1, insofar as a state's right to disenfranchise convicted felons is concerned?

b. May California deny the privileges of an elector to a person convicted of an infamous crime, embezzlement or misappropriation of public money, or exclude from suffrage persons convicted of bribery, perjury, forgery, malfeasance in office, or other high crimes?

Here, Paragraph a is the attention getter, posing the interesting question whether, within the bounds of this great civil rights amendment, there is an unexpected possibility of exclusionary language which may limit the equal protection theme. The possibility of internal constitutional inconsistency may cause the justices to delve further into this case. Paragraph b is the relevant language of the California Constitution stated in question form.

The next section of the brief, Relevant Constitution and Statutes, should give the full text of all constitutional or statutory language which will be referred to in the Argument part. If this is unusually long, it might be beneficial to quote only the vital words and put the rest in the Appendix, provided the rules of your jurisdiction permit this.

"Statement of the Case" comes next. This is a summary of the procedural history of the case: what happened in the courts below to get the case before this appellate court. Some lawyers will mix facts into the Statement of the Case. This really irks the justices. They have to know how the case arose procedurally so they will know how to properly apply rules of law to the facts. Accordingly, the facts should be clearly set forth in a separate section.

The Statement of the Case is prepared from the clerk's transcript of the record: the photocopy of the papers on file in the trial court. Each sentence is carefully referenced to show the page where it may be found. The letters "C.T." indicate it comes from the clerk's transcript. A typical Statement of the Case in a civil matter might look something like this:

On June 27, 1989, appellant brought an action for damages for breach of contract against respondent in the Superior Court of Marlynn County. (C.T.1) On August 7, 1989, the trial court sustained respondent's demurrer without leave to amend. (C.T.54) Judgment for respondent entered December 6, 1989. (C.T.57) Appellant appeals from the Order Sustaining Demurrer Without Leave to Amend. (C.T.59)

Let us look at this for a minute so you will understand what is going on. It will help you to get a clearer background of some of the cases in your casebooks. Assume for a minute that we are one of the justices reading Appellant's Opening Brief. From reading the summary of the procedural activities set out in the Statement of the Case, we have learned that A filed a lawsuit against B, alleging in the Complaint that the parties had entered into a contract, and that B broke the contract. A wants money damages. At this point, we have no idea of the facts. We do know, however, that B filed a Demurrer to the Complaint, a strictly procedural operation, in which B said in effect: "Assuming the facts alleged in the complaint are true, as a matter of law, the complaint fails to state a cause of action."

Because we are only in the Statement of the Case part of the brief so far, and have not yet read the papers in the file or the Statement of Facts, we do not know the grounds for demurrer. But we do have a pretty good idea of what kind of appeal this is: It will be based on some legal or procedural point, rather than an interpretation of facts. Maybe the plaintiff waited too long before filing the lawsuit, and the action was barred by the statute of limitations; or perhaps the alleged facts disclosed that there was no consideration for the contract as a matter of law. As a busy justice, we would go further into the brief rather than speculate.

When you write the next section of the brief, "Statement of Facts," it is extremely important that you be very accurate and limit your description only to those facts set forth in the record on appeal. In Moot Court work, the Statement of Facts will probably be all written out for you.

The information in the Statement of Facts in a real case comes from the reporter's transcript of the trial and the evidence introduced by the parties. If you are writing the Statement of Facts, try to use the exact language of the record as much as possible. If you summarize or paraphrase, stay as close to the original text as grammar will allow.

Remember that you are trying to give the reviewing court a quick picture of a trial that may actually have taken two or three weeks. If a number of witnesses testified to the same thing, you can encapsulate their testimony by using one entry with numerous page citations.

Write the Statement of Facts using a variation on the method you use to prepare for class. First, read the transcript over fast once or twice to get the feel of the case. Witnesses will often testify in an order different from the chronology of events. You will need to know the whole record before you can piece together a logical story.

Try for a reasonably short Statement of Facts. Be sure, however, that you put in enough information to support the legal arguments which follow in the brief. Give the court sufficient facts to permit it to apply the relevant legal issues and rules. To give you an idea of how presentations in briefs may influence justices' decisions, here are two hypothetical partial Statements of Facts in a homicide case, one from the defendant's Appellant's Opening Brief, the other from the prosecution's Respondent's Brief. The letters "R.T." refer to the pages of the Reporter's Transcript of the trial.

A good defense brief writer might look at the evidence this way:

On the afternoon of April 22, 1989, Peter Loring, appellant, was working at the checkout counter of the Lucky Boy Market on Wilson Avenue in Corning. (R.T. pp. 38, 624). Mary Torrent, whom he had known all through high school, was purchasing a whole lot of groceries. (R.T. pp. 42, 198, 630). She said she was putting on a surprise birthday party for Andy Goran.

From here on, R.T. citations will be omitted for clarity. Remember, however, they are necessary after each sentence throughout the briefs so that the justices can turn to the exact place in the record if they want to look more closely at the full testimony on any point.

Peter knew him since they were little kids. They had been good friends, but had drifted apart when Goran started using drugs and dropped out of school in his junior year at Corning High. Goran had become a black leather jacket and chains biker.

Peter took a drink once in a while, but he had seen what dope could do to a guy; how it had wrecked the lives of several of his former classmates. And when he served his tour in Vietnam, he saw a number of guys screw up because of drugs.

Peter and Mary talked for a minute or two—you know how it is at the checkout counter. She left with her groceries. Peter did not see her again until late that night.

After the store closed at 10:00 p.m., Peter and Frank Balba, one of the other checkers, stopped for a beer at the Old Mill Bar. They had two or three bottles apiece and shot some pool. Chuck Turner came in all excited. He had just seen Peter's best friend, Milo Pepper, killed in a fiery explosion when his car was hit by a guy driving on the wrong side of the road across Murphy's Bridge.

Tears came to Peter's eyes. He started drinking straight bourbons. After about an hour or so, Peter was pretty drunk. The bartender eighty-sixed him.

The next thing Peter remembered, he was standing at the table in Mary's living room. Goran was making fun of him because he was crying. When Goran said, "I never liked that Milo Pepper son of a bitch, anyway," Peter felt he wanted to kill him. He started throwing punches. He really wanted to kill him. Goran knocked him to the floor.

Peter left. The only thing he knew was that he wanted to kill Goran because of what he had said about poor Milo Pepper. All he remembers is that he had a knife in his hand. The details are very hazy. Some cop told him he could get a lawyer, that's all.

Here is how the prosecution might present its view of the same evidence:

On April 22, 1989, Mary Torrent gave a surprise birthday party for Andy Goran. Twenty-three guests were invited in addition to Andy. During the evening, appellant, an uninvited person, showed up. He was drunk when he arrived. He kept drinking heavily.

About 1:30 a.m. Andy asked him to leave because he was disturbing the other guests. There was a fist fight between them. Appellant left.

A half hour later appellant appeared at the front door with a long knife. He said, "If you come past this door, you bastard, I'll stick this knife in you."

Andy said nothing and started for the door. Pete Jones and Willie Smith tried to hold him back. Andy brushed them aside and went outside. Everybody followed and made a ring around them. Andy was unarmed.

Appellant said, "I told you I'd stick this knife in you." Andy said, "Go ahead." Appellant lifted the knife. Four of the onlookers rushed to stop him. Appellant stuck the knife into Andy's chest very deeply. The other people pulled him away. Andy fell to the ground.

An ambulance was called. Andy was dead when it arrived.

The police came. They took statements from everybody. Appellant was given his Miranda warning. He said he wanted a lawyer, so there was no further interrogation. He was taken to the county jail.

This example utilizes a subtle prosecution technique which you should be aware of. You will note that nowhere does the appellant's name appear. Yet, at every opportunity, the names of the other witnesses are given. The victim is referred to only once by his full name. After that, he's always called "Andy." Everything has been carefully written to portray the appellant as a nameless, faceless individual. The victim has been personified as much as possible. The idea is to try to get some psychological edge when the reviewing court reads the cold record.

There are two sides to every story, and given the same transcript, there are two ways to tell it. But when you do, do not go outside the record when you write your Statement of Facts. Remember, on appeal the reviewing court is looking for any substantial evidence in that record which will uphold the verdict rendered by the trier of fact. In choosing your facts, do not omit uncontroverted facts which are against you in the hope that the court will not pick them up. And do not select only favorable material so that you distort the record. Always present the facts truthfully and carefully in the best light possible. If you are stuck with a bad fact, mention it if it is important, and continue on.

Just as you should not put any facts into the Statement of the Case, you should not put any arguments into the Statement of Facts. That is what the "Argument" section of the brief is for. There is where you discuss all the issues in the case. The idea is to apply the law to the facts in a persuasive way so that the reviewing court will hand down a decision in your favor.

The argument has to raise legal issues which, from the appellant's point of view, will cause the appellate court to reverse the judgment of the trial court, and from the respondent's point of view, will cause the court to sustain the judgment. In order to find these issues, you have to go through the record looking for possible error. In many jurisdictions, the error must have been pointed out to the trial court by trial counsel, or else it cannot be raised on appeal. Because of constitutional questions relating to due process, equal protection, and right to counsel, however, courts in criminal appeals are more lenient in this regard than with civil litigants.

The question of lack of jurisdiction can generally be raised at any time because, if the trial court had no jurisdiction, it should never have proceeded to judgment in the first instance.

Initially, when looking for issues to develop in the brief, you should go through the clerk's transcript carefully to see if anything shows up in the papers filed in the case which might be of help. Every once in a while an astute lawyer will get a reversal because some elementary requirement was overlooked either before or during trial. When you wrote your Statement of the Case, you probably went through the clerk's transcript a bit superficially, so it is worth this second, more intensive look. Because of the requirement that legal questions must be raised in the trial court in order to be considered on appeal, you may find reported discussions and P's and A's in the record which will more or less frame the scope of the issues you will have to cope with.

If you tried the case, rereading the record will give you a chance to see everything in perspective for the first time. During the trial, you probably were too involved to make impartial observations. If you did not try the case, you can probably be even more objective in evaluating which points might be convincing to the reviewing court.

Before writing your Argument, first outline it so it will read well. Go for the aorta. Put your strongest and most dynamic material right up at the front. Get the justices' attention before you have a chance to lose it. Stick the boring and minor stuff at the end so they can read it after they are almost convinced. Cover everything in whatever depth is necessary, but remember, you are writing a *brief*. Go back to the appellate court clerk's office and look over the briefs that won cases. You will learn a great deal about style, preparation, and argument.

Try to write convincingly. Use legal language, but be careful that you do not get pedantic. Do not drift into colloquialisms. Avoid using contractions; spell everything out. Remember, this is a formal document.

Customarily, the points raised in the Argument are broken down into separate sections, each set off by number, more or less in outline form. Frequently, there are also subsections. Each section and subsection is usually given a title. Put these into the Table of Contents verbatim to give readers a quick look at the scope of your position and to set the proper stage for their perusal. Make your titles as positive as possible. Keep thinking that you have something to sell. Remember that even though the salesperson in the shop shows the customer a lot of merchandise, there is no profit unless the goods move out of the store.

The Argument is followed by the Conclusion. It is a short summary of the major points developed in the brief, plus a clear statement in legal language describing the relief which you are requesting the court to give—for instance, "The Judgment of the Superior Court should be affirmed"; or "The Order Denying Probation should be overruled and the matter referred back to the Superior Court for resentencing."

Any supplementary material should be put in the Appendix. Each item should be separately numbered or lettered as an exhibit to the brief, and should be so noted in the appropriate place in the main text.

The most important thing in brief writing is intensive research and logical argument. It is your work, preparation, and organization which will win or lose the case. While knowledge of the law and insight into its applications are necessarily important, the manner in which your case is presented and argued to a reviewing court can mean the winning or losing on appeal.

20

ENERGIZING THE BRIEF

It always helps if you can find some relevant and unusual historical information to fit into a law review article or a brief, for it whets the reader's intellectual curiosity and frequently can tip the scales of justice in favor of your position. Being aware of the mechanics of good briefing is also useful because it sharpens your awareness of the possibilities for expansion of cases through analogy. And it helps you think of new ways to attack problems.

Here is an interesting situation that occurred in a criminal appellate case I handled some years ago. The defendants had been convicted of "conspiracy to injure the public health." In their opening brief, their counsel argued that the charge was so broad and vague as to be constitutionally void.

In criminal law, you will learn that every defendant has the right to know specifically what the charge is so that a proper defense can be prepared. If the language of the indictment or information is not clear enough for a reasonable person to understand that the conduct complained of is criminal, the charging document is insufficient as a matter of law, and the case must be dismissed. Since this goes to the very heart of the jurisdiction of the court to try the case, it is an issue which can be raised for the first time on appeal. It need not be raised in the original trial.

In this matter, intensive research on both sides failed to come up with a case in any Anglo-American jurisdiction which had ever defined the phrase "injury to the public health." The very logical defense argument was that since this language had never been defined anywhere, either by case or statute, it was impossible for someone to know beforehand whether the acts to be entered upon would constitute a crime. In constitutional law, this theory is referred to as the "void for vagueness doctrine."

In briefing the state's case, since there was no precedent to follow, I had to try another approach. You will recall that the common law of the United States includes all the law of England, both statutes and cases, that existed as of the time of the signing of the Declaration of Independence, in 1776. I decided to trace this conspiracy statute back to see if there was any indication of how it came to be enacted.

When you are analyzing a statute, always write it out in longhand. It is amazing how certain words will suddenly take on new meaning, how punctuation becomes critical, how the very style of the statutory language can cause new ideas to form in your mind—ideas which may give you some clue to the solution of the problem at hand. That is what happened to me in this case. I found that the statute was enacted by the First Legislature of California. The style looked suspiciously as if it had been copied from somewhere else. There was too much detail for it to have been created out of thin air. I got out the statute book for that First Legislature. It was part of a whole enactment devoted to criminal law; it was part of an entire criminal code. My speculation was that some lawyer might have come out in the 1849 gold rush and brought his law books along just in case he did not strike it rich as a miner. Perhaps he was elected a member of the First Legislature and proposed a bill which incorporated the criminal code used in his home state.

A little research showed that I was possibly on the right track. The current New York statute on conspiracy was almost word for word the same as California's. I was able to trace the New York law back to 1829 but could not find any similar language predating it. So I thought it might be possible to pick something up if I started at the beginning and worked forward instead of backward.

The rare book section of the library gave me what I was looking for. I scanned the indices of all New York statutes from the time the English took over Manhattan Island from the Dutch. There was nothing useable on conspiracy in any index. However, I spotted a word that looked enticing: "chirurgion."

Earlier in this book, I suggested that you read as broadly as possible because you never know when some little bit of information will be helpful. That is what happened here. Years before, I had come across an article on the origin of red-and-white striped barber poles which claimed they originated in Germany. Because of their intimate knowledge of knife sharpening, barbers also conducted a sideline business in surgery. The poles outside their shops were painted white to match the plastered walls of their buildings. When the rags used to wipe up the blood were washed, they were draped around the poles to facilitate drying. These precursors of present day surgeons were called "chirurgeons."

This turned out to be the clue I was looking for. Here is how it came out in the brief:

THE MEANING OF THE TERM "INJURY TO THE PUBLIC HEALTH" HAS BEEN WELL KNOWN TO THE COMMON LAW FOR HUNDREDS OF YEARS

The meaning of the term "injury to the public health" has been well known to the common law for several hundred years. It goes back to the very foundation of the Colony of New York in 1664 when the English took over Manhattan Island from the Dutch.

The Duke of York's Laws for the Government of the Colony of New York were compiled under the direction of the first governor, Richard Nicolls, from existing laws for the government of other English colonies in America. The following statute, sandwiched somewhat alphabetically amidst titles such as "churchwardens," "charges publicke," "children and servants," and material relating to courts, goes right to the heart of "injury to the public health." It became effective in 1665.

CHIRURGIONS, MIDWIVES, PHYSICIANS

That no Person or Persons whatsoever, Employed about the Bed of Men women or Children at any time for the preservation of Life or health as Chirurgions, Midwives, Physicians or others; presume to Exercise or put forth any Acte Contrary to the known approved Rules of Art in each mistery or Occupation, or exercise any force, violence or Cruelty upon, or to the Bodies of any whether Young or old; without the advice and Councell of the such as are Skillfull in the same Art (If such may be had,) or at least of some of the wisest and gravest when present and Consent of the patient or patients if they be Mentis Compotes: much less Contrary to such Advice and Consent upon such severe punishments as the nature of the fault may deserve, which Law nevertheless is not intended to discourage any from all Lawfull use of their skill but rather to encourage and direct them in the right use thereof, and to inhibit and restrain the presumptious arogancy of such as through Confidence of their own skill, or any sinister Respect, dare bouldly attempt to Exercise any violence upon or toward the body of young or old one or other, to the prejudice or hazard of the Life or Limb of man, woman or child." Vol. 1, The Colonial Laws of New York from the Year 1664 to the Revolution, pp. 6, 27.

In 1755, New York enacted its first law setting up a ship quarantine area to curtail the spread of infections and contagious diseases. Van Shaak's Laws, ch. 973; 3 Colonial Laws of New York, 1071.

In 1760, the New York Colonial Legislature passed an act to restrain quacks practicing in the City of New York, which act provided for examination and licensing of physicians and surgeons, and provided monetary penalties for practicing without the certification.

The preamble of that act provided:

"WHEREAS many ignorant and unskilful Persons in Physick and Surgery in order to gain a Subsistence do take upon themselves to administer Physick and practice Surgery in the City of New York to the endangering of the Lives and Limbs of their Patients; and many poor and ignorant Persons inhabiting the said City who have been persuaded to become their Patients have been great sufferers thereby: For preventing such Abuses for the future. . . . " 4 Colonial Laws of New York, 455, 1180.

In 1806, the New York State Legislature passed the first medical society act and turned over the examination and licensing of doctors to the profession. The act provided for expulsion of members, if necessary, and that other than grandfather clause practioners could not thereafter practice unless certified by the society. Laws of New York, 29th Session, ch. 138.

It is submitted that the term "any act injurious to the public health" was a well defined phrase at common law and specifically was directed toward (1) quarantine violations, and (2) unnecessary operations and unlicensed practice of medicine which had for their motives avarice and greedy expectation of financial gain or other sinister purposes.

It is also persuasive to note that when the conspiracy statute was initially enacted, everything, after the initial language relating to commission of any offense, was directed to crimes revolving around fraud. And fraud obviously was one of the sinister purposes for which doctors could have been severely punished under the Duke of York Laws and later colonial laws relating to unlicensed practice of medicine.

Finally, the great concern of government that its citizens must be protected from intentional acts obviously injurious to the public health is reflected in the fact that both the Duke of York Laws and the original California statute were each promulgated or enacted at the very time the respective governments were first being established: in New York right after the surrender of the Dutch; in California right after admission of the state.

By the time of oral argument, I found more material in a little book entitled *His Majesty's Laws for the Plantations of Delaware and Pennsylvania*. Accompanied by an armed library bailiff, I brought that rare old volume to court with me. You should have seen the justices delicately turning the brittle pages. If you are interested, you can read the entire decision in *People* v. *Rehman*, 253 Cal. App. 2d 119, 61 Cal. Rep. 65. You will not often have the opportunity to play around with legal history in such depth, but when conditions are ripe you can have a lot of fun and satisfaction.

21

WHAT KIND OF LAW
WILL YOU PRACTICE?

Most law students plan to practice a particular type of law after they graduate. Unfortunately, reality soon interferes with dreams. Unlike television shows, where the scriptwriters can program their characters into the most exciting legal situations, the individual attorney often has to take what comes along, and in most cases finds involvement working in areas never envisioned during law school.

A law practice evolves from the needs of the clients, not the aspirations of the lawyer. The clients pay the rent. You may have the potential to be the greatest trial lawyer who ever trod the boards of the bar, but if you accidentally happen to fall into a series of uncontested divorces at several thousand dollars a crack, you will quickly find that is where your expertise and reputation will develop. Each happy divorced person you represent will be a walking ad testifying to your prowess, and each fee you collect will involve you more deeply into your newfound specialty. Once in a while you will get that big trial which you initially envisioned you would have every day of your career; but do not look for it too often. Or it may happen the other way around. Perhaps you wanted to be a big divorce lawyer, yet you find yourself in court every day defending cases for some insurance company. If you do get what you looked forward to, consider yourself extremely lucky—most of your colleagues will be less fortunate.

Some people find that they cannot adjust to practicing a different kind of law from what they dreamed of, and they drift out of the profession. Others discover that the work they always hoped to do, which once looked so glamorous and exciting, becomes drab and even distasteful when they have to make a living at it. They, too, float away.

If you discover that you are one of these unfortunate persons who have a problem practicing law, start thinking right away about changing to another area. It is not the end of the world, and there is no stigma in going into something else. On the other hand, to spend your life at something you are not happy with, when there are other alternatives, is certainly not a desirable situation.

What types of law are open to the new graduate? Essentially, there are three main ways to go: working for yourself, either alone or in association with others; working for someone else, such as a law firm or a legal clinic; and working for an institution such as government, a corporation, a poverty law group, or in a law school teaching post.

For years, the "big deal" in American law schools has been to see how many of the top ranking graduates can get placed as associates with the prestigious gigantic law firms, or receive clerkships with state and federal appellate court justices and federal district court judges. That is practically all the professors and students talk about when job placement is discussed, because these jobs traditionally lead to big money.

The large firms have so much business that they have to hire lawyers to do the work without worrying whether these people bring in any new clients. The work is arduous, the hours are long, and the pay is good. In years past, a competent, hard-working lawyer with one of these firms could expect to become a partner within a reasonable number of years. Today, this expectation is clouded. Big firms have found themselves overcrowded with partners, and there have been quite a few tales lately about infighting and disagreements relating to allocation of profits. Some old, established organizations have split up in public acrimony. Some firms have even established two-track career lines, one leading to partner, one to high-salaried expert associate. Partners in the large firms get six-figure annual salaries, and frequently also receive stock in corporate clients as partial payment for their services.

Young lawyers who get judicial clerkships gain tremendous knowledge and experience as they work up complicated cases for their justices and observe the lawyers of the community in daily practice before the courts. After a few years, they frequently leave for private practice with one of the good medium-size or smaller law firms. Their work for the courts gives them great exposure to the successful members of the bar. Here too, as in the big firms, they are associated because there is too much work for existing members of the firm to handle. Over the years, they build up their own clientele and either bring that with them into the partnership or go into practice for themselves.

If you get on a corporate legal staff, you will be on a course leading to an eventual vice-presidency in charge of the law department. Rarely will you get any trial work of consequence; most of the time that is contracted out to outside counsel. Mostly, you will handle interpretation of agreements, negotiations and preventive type legal advice. The advancement timetable is relatively slow; you may have to wait for the people ahead of you to get promoted, retire or die. The pay is usually good, the hours are better, the fringe benefits are excellent, and the responsibility increases with your years of service. Among the drawbacks are the frequent use of outside counsel to second-guess your important opinions, and the ever-present possibility that some group of outsiders will take over the corporation and squeeze you out.

There are not too many law school teaching positions open. If you manage to obtain one, you will most likely fall victim to the "publish or perish" syndrome. You will undoubtedly have to bounce around from school to school before you get tenure. Salaries are not too bad; that long summer vacation is something no one else in the business has; and as you become known in your field, there is a good opportunity to do consultant work on the side.

Some of the poverty or public interest law firms pay fairly well, but many of them seem to think that you should be paying for the privilege of representing their clients. Responsibility comes early and fast. You may get numerous tiny cases or *big class* actions with great social implications. But they are your cases. Much of the time, because of the heavy workload, there is no one else around to handle them. Opportunity to go into trial and appellate courts is frequent. A lot of lawyers gain their early experience in these firms and then move out into private practice.

Working for a government agency has many compensations. There is a steady progression of promotions; the pay is adequate, although seldom as high as in big private-sector law firms, but fairly close to the incomes of private practitioners; the fringe benefits and vacations are good; retirement programs are generally excellent; responsibility comes quickly and heavily.

In the federal government area, most entrants get into large agencies where they handle administrative law, house counsel advisory work, statutory drafting and interpretation, and similar activities. The work is often not exciting; the hours are not overtaxing. On the other hand, if you are with the United States attorney general's office, you go into trial and appellate courts to represent the other governmental departments. In a local United States attorney's office, you handle criminal and civil trials. With the federal public defender, you do straight criminal defense work for indigent clients accused of offenses against the United States. Long hours are balanced by the zest inherent in the work.

At the state levels, there are the attorney general's offices. Most of the criminal work is at the appellate level; however, sometimes when a county district attorney cannot handle a local case for some reason or another, a deputy state attorney general is sent to fill in. The civil work, which usually is much more voluminous, consists of advising state agencies, issuing written opinions, and representing the state and its officials in administrative law matters or when they sue or are sued in their official capacities. Where there is a state public defender's office, the work consists mainly of writing briefs and arguing the cases on appeal. Again, as in all these active legal offices, there are lots of long hours enhanced by exciting cases.

County district attorney and public defender positions are similar. You work just as hard, but the pay is usually lower. These positions give you fantastic experience in trying criminal cases at every level.

County counsel spots, generally at the same salary as the district attorney's, take care of all the civil law business for the county. Some city attorney's offices will give similar experience, but there are few jobs because most cities retain part-time outside private practitioners to handle this work.

Individuals who are lucky enough to get several years of solid trial experience in a district attorney's office, followed by some years of intensive civil law experience in a county counsel's office, usually wind up as very successful private practitioners in their local communities. This is because during their years of public service they receive a great deal of favorable local publicity in newspapers and on television. Also, because the lawyers in the county counsel's office do much of their work as opponents of the monied interests—landowners, ranchers, business owners, developers, and so forth—their abilities are highly visible and respected; and when one of these persons wants to change attorneys, a former assistant county counsel now in private practice looks like just the lawyer to have on retainer to handle complex problems.

A common factor separating all these institutional positions from jobs with small or medium-sized law firms is compensation based on worth. The government, for example, does not have the overhead problems of the small firm; it does not have to exploit you, intentionally or otherwise, to keep you on the payroll.

If you do not make a connection with any of the above groups, then you have the choice of working for one of the smaller firms or opening your own shop. One of the big problems to be aware of is the tendency for a vast number of medium and small firms to take in a young lawyer with the promise (usually honest, but sometimes not) that a partnership will result "if things work out." Many times, however, it does not. The young lawyer feels exploited because of long hours and low pay; the firm feels that there has not been enough work product for the money expended, and they part with hard feelings on both sides. The lawyer gets another job, the firm hires some other new person, and the same thing happens over again. Eventually, the lawyer associates with some other lawyers who have had similar experiences, or practices alone.

Let us take a look at the economics of this small firm employment situation, assuming good faith in the initial hiring. Say they give you x dollars a month to start. It is almost a certainty that they will have to lay out another x dollars to pay for your office space, furniture, telephone, secretary, medical benefits, social security and unemployment taxes, and malpractice insurance. They have spent $2x$ dollars on you before you have brought in a penny. The work you do will have to bring in twice your salary for them simply to break even.

Since the firm is in business to make money, they will expect you to work still harder at the same pay so that they can recoup more from your billable time to the clients. Also, since you are new, you will be working slower than someone with experience. Without your realizing it, or their explaining it, they will feel that you need to put in $3x$ hours of hard work to earn $1x$ hours of pay. It is pretty obvious that there is no way they can take you in as a partner unless you bring in enough business to put you up there in the proprietary class with them—business that you have to share with them until that time because you are using their facilities to take care of it.

Now let us see what happens if you start working for yourself right from the beginning. Every penny you take in is yours. True, you have to pay for your overhead before you can pay yourself, but once that is taken care of, you are ahead as far as you can go. The biggest thrill you will ever get in the law business is the day you get your first big fee which is free and clear of any expenses, and which you know is all yours. The greatest additional compensation from self-employment, one which you cannot put any money value on, is the knowledge that you are your own boss. You call the shots. You give the clients the advice which you know is correct. You handle the cases your way. If you do not like the looks or ethics of a client, you do not have to take the case.

But where do you get the clients? Don't you have to work for someone else to make a living? In the next chapters, I will give you a different perspective on this.

Even though you cannot really know what type of practice you will be headed for, it is a good idea to keep your desires in mind when you choose electives. Until a few years ago, the law school curriculum was pretty rigid and standardized for the entire three years. Today, you have the opportunity to do a lot of exploration.

What kind of electives should you choose? If your grades are really good and it looks like you might be headed for one of those big law firm or judicial clerkship jobs, you might want to opt for courses like Advanced Trusts and Estates, Advanced Federal Practice, or Advanced Federal Taxation. On the other hand, if you know you are probably headed for general practice, take those courses which will pay off quickest: Advanced Criminal Procedure, Family Law Practice, Advanced Civil Procedure, or Trial Tactics. Most students take many of the same electives, but if you look carefully at what is offered, you may pick up some very valuable knowledge.

22

WHERE ARE YOU GOING TO PRACTICE?

When it comes time to decide where to start practicing, look for a place where you believe you will enjoy the community surroundings and feel secure living among the people who are already there. This is a must. Over the years, as you progress in your practice, you will become an important member of this group; and if you want to enjoy the life, you will have to fit in and accept the local customs. Of course, where you practice is partially based on where you get a job offer. But keep the community question in mind, and if you have serious doubts, do not go there.

Check to see if there are any states where you can be admitted to the bar without further examination if you already are a member in another state. The list changes from time to time, and with the use of the National Bar Examination new areas may be opening up.

If you are going to start by opening your own office, remember that a law practice is based on people. The more people you know who think of you as a lawyer, the more clients you will have. If you have a big family and many friends somewhere, give serious consideration to opening up there. You will have a built-in referral system that should pay off fairly quickly, and the familiar surroundings will require less personal adjustment.

When I first looked for a place to practice in California, far from my original home, family and friends, I sent a detailed résumé of my background to the presiding judge of each superior court in the state, along with a letter asking about the opportunities for practice in the county. Surprisingly, I received a personal response from each one of them, some fairly long, giving much valuable information. Some judges gave me a run-down on the various firms, a few suggested places where there might be job openings, and one even told me of an office for rent where a recently deceased lawyer had practiced for over twenty years. The most interesting was from a judge who wrote that a young lawyer starting out could do very well in his county "if there was a willingness to compromise oneself and be a whore for the lumber industry."

Additionally, I studied Audit Bureau of Circulation reports, chamber of commerce publications, census records and telephone yellow pages at the library for detailed background on the various places in the state. I traveled around so I could physically inspect areas and cities and personally talk to practicing lawyers and other persons in the communities: storekeepers, teachers, clergy, police officers, elected officials, and others.

You never know what you are going to run into. I once visited a beautiful mountain agricultural area with only 1,500 people living in the county seat. At a big ranch where I stopped to chat, I was invited to lunch. The rancher and his wife were delightful, well-educated people. They told me that this particular small county had about 40 percent college graduates and about 10 percent had advanced degrees. In their opinion, a new lawyer would have a difficult time because most of the monied people in the community used lawyers in a large city about one hundred miles distant.

I asked about their cultural interests. They replied that that evening, for example, the county amateur symphony society was meeting in their barn; he played the bassoon and she played the cello. There were two book discussion groups every month, a scientific forum, and lots more. This place sounded so good that I almost forgot that I would have to make a living, and I gave it serious thought for awhile.

Within a couple of weeks, I began to get a feeling of where I would probably settle. Finally, everything merged, and four cities stood out as ideal locations. I picked one, and over the years, was extremely satisfied that I had made a proper choice. Later on, when I was doing well, other lawyers in the community often suggested that neophytes looking for a place to light see me for ideas. Whenever I could make the time, I would talk to them. Many lawyers will do the same. It is a chance to relax for a few minutes and extend the hand of friendship to a new member of the fraternity.

One such visit was with a young lawyer who was single and free to go practically anywhere. We talked about the two hundred lawyers in my court "trading area," the most common types of practice, usual overhead expenses, fees charged, chances for success, and so on. We also discussed the cultural activities available, organizations he might consider joining, nearby recreational activities, and the like. Our conversation turned to a dam scheduled for construction in about six months. It was up in the mountains, some 30 miles from nowhere. The only businesses at the moment were a crossroads country store and a bar. A survey crew living in a couple of trailers added to the small population. But once work on the dam started, there would be thousands of construction people in the area. I suggested he consider renting a small piece of ground and building a two-room law office up there, right outside where the main gate would be. Neither of us knew whether it would prove to be any good, but he left the meeting intrigued with the possibilities.

Doing most of the work himself, he erected an Abraham Lincoln–type wooden shack, complete with porch and a swinging sign bearing his name and the word "Lawyer." For four or five months, as expected, he did not get much business. Even during that period, however, he did pick up some small contract work and drew a will for one of the local farmers. Then came the inundation. Work on the dam started. Overnight, thousands of construction workers passed his office every day. He was the only lawyer for miles around. And all his clients had ready cash.

Individuals who had been arrested over the weekend for being
drunk or fighting in town paid him a fee to appear in court and pay
the fine. A personal appearance would have meant loss of a day's
pay. There were divorces, wills, industrial compensation cases, auto
accidents, leases—an entire general practice. Suddenly, this newly
practicing lawyer was doing better than many of the attorneys who
had been around the county seat for a lot longer.

A few years later, as the dam was nearing completion, he stopped
by my office to tell me he was moving away to a neighboring state
and was going to get married. I asked why he did not bring his bride
down here instead. With a chuckle, he replied, "They're building a
new dam up there."

While it is nice to be able to start practice with a fine library,
leather furniture, and a top-notch secretary, it is quite possible to get
along with less. Many of today's successful lawyers started practice
without even the proverbial nickel. If they had no books, they put
up law school casebooks. A few may have told their clients that they
practiced "unwritten law." Others may have suggested that they
never let the authorities prejudice their viewpoints. Most probably
said they were just starting out and did their research over at the
county law library at the courthouse. For the bookshelves they did
need, they used stained boards propped up on cinder blocks. For
furniture, they got secondhand pieces and refinished them at home.
Many did their own typing until they could afford to hire someone.

When I was going to New York University just before World War
II, the Great Depression was still on, and I had a chance to observe
the most extreme shoestring law practices in operation. Sad though
it is to reflect upon, it does illustrate how some enterprising individuals in the worst of times were able to continue to practice law and
manage to squeeze out a living for themselves and their families.
About 50 lawyers hung around Grand Central Station all day—that
was their office. Each had cards printed up with name, post office
box number, and the telephone number of a pay phone in the
station which always had an "Out of Order" sign hanging on it.
When a call came in, the nearest lawyer would answer, "Law offices."
When the client gave the name of his lawyer, that person would be
called to the telephone. After talking to his client, the lawyer would

go to his file, a cardboard box kept in a dime-a-day luggage locker. He typed his letters and pleadings on a rental typewriter nearby.

I hope such severe challenges to legal ingenuity will never again arise. But the point to remember out of all this is, that even if you start small, if you have the desire to practice law and the fortitude to hang in for a while, there is a good chance that you will succeed.

Today, with computers and applicable software, and an answering machine to take your messages, it is fairly easy to start a do-it-yourself law office. Law book companies are happy to give you a line of credit if you want to fill the shelves. Be careful, however, that you do not overbuy because the monthly payments seem so low.

There are many sources of leads on jobs, association possibilities, and places to practice. For example, at county seats throughout the country the little newspapers specializing in real estate and court news contain legal notices, court filings and calendars, and often advertisements for legal positions. In the large cities there are legal newspapers loaded with columns of ads for lawyers wanted, not only in those cities, but all over that state and other areas as well. Many students and graduates will, of course, use the law school placement office. But they also graduated as undergraduates from a college. Recently, I spoke with a new lawyer who neglected this resource because there was no law school where she got her B.A. When she checked back with them, she found that several alumni were looking for lawyers who had gone there. She wound up on the legal staff of a fairly large computer corporation whose president was a fellow graduate.

Generally, the bigger the city, the better the possibility for a high salary. The centers of industry and commerce attract the larger law firms and create the volume of business which allows more money to be paid to new lawyers.

In the smaller communities, several established firms usually control most of the good law practice in the area. They represent most of the larger businesses and wealthier people. The senior partners in these firms have long-established, interlocking, rooted family connections. They are the lawyers who pull the power strings, work behind the scenes, and control the policies of the major governmental and other institutions in the community. But there is always room in these places for a good young solo practitioner to handle cases against the establishment firms. A few victories in court, or well handled negotiations, will soon make the older lawyers aware of fresh talent in town, and quite often, when they have something which they cannot handle in their own offices, they will refer a client to someone whom they can trust to reflect favorably on their recommendation.

23

HOW TO GET CLIENTS

If you join a corporation, government, or some other organization where your paycheck comes in regularly, you will not have to worry about how to get clients. But if you are considering opening up on your own, or are going with a firm that expects you to bring in business, this chapter is especially for you.

Earlier, I discussed the economics of exploitation of young lawyers. If it looks like you are getting into that kind of bind, you might give serious thought to working for yourself. Rather than working long hours at low pay for someone else, you might be much better off putting all that energy into something you were developing for yourself.

A good time to start is when you just get out of law school. Most likely, you will be single then, and other than perhaps a big loan to repay, you really do not have many obligations. If things are a little tough in the beginning, remember that the potential is great. Start thinking about a place to practice as early as possible. Even a year or more before graduation is not too soon. Look over various locations in light of what I outlined in the last chapter. Get the best office your finances will permit. If you have money, be sure to set some aside to carry you for at least a year. If you have none, you have little to lose.

I am not suggesting that you go into something as serious as this without doing some deep thinking, but I do want to point out that the problem is not insurmountable.

If you do some careful budget planning, and write up a detailed formal business plan, you may be able to borrow money from a local branch bank to help you get started. If you can convince the banker that you have a future, and are convinced yourself that it really is there, you are a good candidate for a loan. If the bank has invested in you, there is a good chance that it will refer business to you. The busier you are, the more secure the loan is. Every day, bank customers ask their bankers to recommend a good lawyer for some problem they need handled. Additionally, the bank has a lot of small business which its regular counsel is not set up to take care of properly. For example, there are a number of guardianships under various state and federal programs which require annual accountings to be filed in the local county court. For propriety, the bank prefers to be represented by independent counsel when it asks for a fee out of its ward's guardianship estate. Sometimes the relative of a deceased depositor will ask the bank to act as administrator of the estate when there is no will. In that case, the trust officer of the bank has the discretion to choose the lawyer to handle the case in court.

Be sure to send out announcements to all your relatives, friends and acquaintances. As soon as you pass the bar, you will receive mail solicitations from printing companies offering package deals for announcements, letterheads, cards, billforms, and so on, which can get you started.

One student I knew was certain she would be opening her own office right after she was admitted to practice. All through law school she kept a card index of practically everyone she ever met or did business with, even down to the checkers at the supermarket. When she sent out her announcements, she took the time to add some little handwritten personal note to each one, such as, "Still remember that pleasant talk we had at Jan and Bill's open house last fall. Drop in and say Hi." She never solicited business, but so many people appreciated her friendly manner that she got a number of them as her clients, and many more referred clients to her. Within a fairly short time she was running a successful law practice.

You never know where clients will come from. My first client is a good example. It was right after World War II. When I opened my office, I had few tangible assets. My wife, my young son and I were living in veterans' housing that had been converted from officers' quarters at a recently closed air base about twenty miles out of town. We had no car. Anxious to get to work early on the first day, I got out on the highway about 6:00 A.M., long before the first bus, and wearing my blue suit and carrying my empty briefcase, took the Thumb and Shoeleather Line to the office.

A friendly elderly farmer in a pickup stopped and gave me a lift. He asked what I was doing all dressed up so far out of town. At first he could not believe that I was really a lawyer. Then, after we talked awhile, he said he admired my determination and asked me to give him some cards so he could send me some business. I carefully gave him one, from the hundred I had received in the special mail-order stationery packet, hoarding the rest for later rationing to other potential clients. But he wanted a lot. Three were not enough; five were not enough. Finally, ten satisfied him. As he let me off in front of my building, he wished me luck and said I would definitely be hearing from him.

To say things were slow at the office that day would be the essence of understatement. When I called my wife at noon, I put on a brave front so she would not be discouraged. Although no one had been in yet, there were still five hours to go. And then, at exactly 4:00 P.M., the door opened, and in walked a straw-hatted, Levi-jeaned, cowboy-booted man accompanied by a heavy-set, heavily made-up lady in a low-cut flowered dress.

"I want to buy my girlfriend a divorce, and my boss said he met you this morning and you were the lawyer to go see to get it done."

After a discussion in which I obtained the necessary information and explained the procedure and length of time it would take, we got to the matter of the fee. I quoted the minimum suggested by the local Bar Association schedule, expecting to get a retainer, with the balance to be paid when the services were completed. To my pleasant shock, he took out a roll of bills and paid cash for the whole thing. It was more than enough to pay all the office expenses for a month. I was on my way.

153

Some lawyers go the organization route. They join every society or group that will take them in. Because of their training and experience, they quickly get on committees and soon become officers. The weekly meeting exposure and status make the members remember that they are lawyers, and it is rare someone does not come up and ask some legal question. Most of this banter is for free; however, quite a bit turns into something which brings in a client to the office.

An excellent source of business is teaching a "Law for Laymen" course at an evening high school or community college. Although a lot of students are really trying to get advice about their own problems, your answers to their questions, and the very fact that you are the expert giving the lecture, makes you the great oracle. Most will come to you professionally when they have a serious problem and will also tell all their friends and relatives what a great lawyer you are.

At the risk of overindulgence, a lawyer who hits the bars selectively every night on the way home from the office picks up a lot of business. One might go to the same bar and stay for a couple of hours, buying drinks and just being a good guy. Another will go to three or four, staying for a drink at each. Regulars at bars seem to need lawyers more often than most, or have friends and acquaintances who do, and thus are the source of many referrals.

The church lawyers achieve the same end in an entirely different way. They and their wives are heavily into less "profane" activities, and because of the high status and respect they receive, the congregants look to them as the only lawyers to go to when legal problems arise.

Some lawyers get their clients from people they meet jogging; some from playing golf. It does not seem to matter as long as the lawyer is in a place where a number of people over a period of time become used to the idea that "this person is a lawyer, and if I need one, or know someone who does, I will recommend this person to handle the problem."

Since the Supreme Court has declared that all persons charged with felonies must be provided with lawyers if they cannot afford them, many counties now have public defenders who handle cases for indigents. Frequently, there is a need for additional counsel to represent a codefendant because of possible conflict of interest between them. This means that the court must appoint an outside attorney at county expense. Besides the money you will get from these cases, the experience is invaluable. These people are your clients, just like the others you get in the normal course of business. Along similar lines, check into whether you can be appointed to represent a criminal defendant on appeal. Many states pay appointed counsel to prepare and argue the briefs in those cases.

A number of lawyers prepare income tax returns for their clients. Often this is the first contact many people have with a lawyer. Many will need wills prepared in the future, or will need other legal services during the year.

Do not overlook the word-of-mouth advertising you can get from your present clients. I once drew a will for traveling salesman as he was passing through town. He asked me to keep the original in my safe, but wondered how his relatives would know about it if anything happened to him while he was on the road. I gave him a couple of my cards to send to one or two of them, and also gave him one to keep in his wallet. Each had the following message typed on the back: "In case of accident, serious illness, or death, please contact my lawyer named on the other side of this card."

Beginning about three weeks later, I started getting a steady stream of new clients from all over the state. It seems they would mention some legal problem in the course of a conversation, and this salesman would suggest that they see his lawyer, who was so concerned about his welfare that he had him keep this card in his wallet just in case anything happened to him.

Another time, a man and a woman came in to have a partnership agreement prepared. One had a lease on a piece of ground, the other had the equipment necessary to cultivate it. They wanted "a partnership without clauses." What they meant, of course, was an agreement which an ordinary layperson could readily understand. I prepared something in simple language which started out like this: "Mary Smith and Charlie Jones want to form a partnership to grow corn. Mary has the lease on eighty acres at the corner of Marshall and Bradshaw Roads. . . ." The completed document did not have any whereases, therefores, parties of the first part, or other wording which many people think is necessary "to make it really legal.' All the required elements of a partnership were there, but in language which was completely intelligible to them. Word soon got around, and I achieved some local fame as the lawyer who could draw "partnerships without clauses." This one agreement led to almost fifty like it each year drawn for people who wanted "plain talk."

When people wanted extra copies of wills to send to relatives, I gladly supplied them. Frequently the recipients came into the office with business of their own. This once had interesting repercussions. An old pensioner I knew came in for a will. He told me that he had lived very frugally for the last ten years and had been able to put a little bit of money into the stock market each month. His investments had paid off big and he now had over $200,000 on deposit in several savings and loan accounts. He wanted to divide it all among seven nephews and nieces. I prepared the will and, at his request, sent copies to each of the relatives named. Some months later, he left the community.

A few years passed. He showed up smoking a good cigar and dressed in a fairly nice suit. He said one of his nieces had given him one that no longer fit her husband. He then told me that he had lied about the money on deposit in the banks; he really never had a dime. But he had been visiting each of the seven nephews and nieces on a rotation basis and life had really been great. Each of them had been trying to outdo the others in hospitality, always hinting that it would be nice to get a larger share of his estate.

Be aware of the subtle positive effect professional certificates hanging on the walls of your office can have on your clients. Did you ever hear someone say, "My attorney is admitted to practice before the Supreme Court of the United States"? I will let you in on a little secret. Any lawyer who has been admitted to practice in any state for three years or more, and who is in good standing, can become a member of the Bar of the United States Supreme Court merely by filling out an application obtained from the Clerk of the Court, having the admission proposed by two other lawyers who are members, and sending in the required fee. In the old days, it was necessary to actually go to Washington, attend a session, and take the oath administered by the Chief Justice. Today, it can all be done by mail. When you get your three years in, get your certificate. Even if you have do not have your own office, at the very least your parents will be proud.

To fill up your walls, you can get all kinds of certificates admitting you to practice before various federal administrative agencies. Check them out.

Some years ago, in the exercise of a hobby to temporarily get away from the daily stress of practicing law, I carved a statue out of redwood, "Supreme Court in Action," a cast of which is now in the Supreme Court Museum in Washington. I gave one to Chief Justice Earl Warren, who I understand kept it in his chambers until his death. My own cast was proudly on display in my office until I retired from practice. It bears an engraved plate in the center giving the date of my admission to the Supreme Court Bar. Also, there are four smaller plates, each listing the name of one of the cases I argued before the Court.

A number of lawyers throughout the county, even though they have not actually argued, also have casts in their offices. While the statue is exhibited as an art piece, it does quietly direct clients' attention to their admission in a dignified manner.

When you do get admitted to the Supreme Court, and you happen to be in Washington, go to the Court library and register as one of the members of the Bar. This gives you access to the privileges of that library, and you can use it for research while you are in town. Check with the librarian for futher details and benefits.

Running for some political office gives you terrific name recognition, and whether you win or lose, your supporters usually remain very loyal to you and refer clients for a long time after the election has passed.

If you have the money to spend, paid advertising can be quite rewarding; however, check this out carefully. Many lawyers do not believe it brings results unless you have a big budget for the ads.

Whatever method you adopt for attracting clients, choose one that fits your personality. You should be comfortable with both your methods and the clients you obtain by them. The group you appeal to will be the basis of your law practice. May good fortune follow you as you wend your way through law school and the bar exam into many happy years of practice.

SELECTED LAW REVIEW READINGS

NOTE: There are various ways of citing law review articles, depending on how they are being used. Below they are printed in standard bibliographical form. Technical legal writing customarily follows the method set forth in *A Uniform System of Citation*, published by The Harvard Law Review Association, with the author's name in regular roman type, the title of the article in italics, and the name of the law review in large and small capital letters. In the *Index to Legal Periodicals* everything is set in regular type; however, the volume, page, and year appear at the end of the citation, with the volume and page separated by a colon and the year being abbreviated.

ADMINISTRATIVE LAW

Carrow, "Types of Judicial Relief from Administrative Action," 58 *Colum. L. Rev.* 1 (1958).

Freedman, "Summary Action by Administrative Agencies," 40 *U. Chi. L. Rev.* 1 (1972).

Stewart, "The Reformation of American Administrative Law," 88 *Harv. L. Rev.* 1669 (1975).

Zamir, "Administrative Control of Administrative Action," 57 *Calif. L. Rev.* 866 (1969).

AGENCY

Seavey, "Subagents and Subservants," 68 *Harv. L. Rev.* 658 (1954).

COMMERCIAL LAW

Benson and Squillante, "Role of the Holder in Due Course Doctrine in Consumer Credit Transactions," 26 *Hastings L. J.* 427 (1974).

Danzig, "A Comment on the Jurisprudence of the Uniform Commercial Code," 27 *Stan. L. Rev.* 621 (1975).

Friedman, "Formative Elements in the Law of Sales: The Eighteenth Century," 44 *Minn. L. Rev.* 363 (1960).

Llewellyn, "Across Sales on Horseback," 52 *Harv. L. Rev.* 725 (1939).

Llewellyn, "The First Struggle to Unhorse Sales," 52 *Harv. L. Rev.* 873 (1939).

Palmer, "Negotiable Instruments under the Uniform Commercial Code," 48 *Mich. L. Rev.* 255 (1950).

Schmitt and Johnson, "A Poker Player's Guide to Uniform Commercial Code Secured Transactions," 10 *Sw. U. L. Rev.* 2089 (1978).

"Uniform Commercial Code," 16 *Law and Contemp. Prob.* 1-346 (1951).

CONFLICT OF LAWS

Barrett, "The Doctrine of Forum Non Conveniens," 35 *Calif. L. Rev.* 380 (1947).

Cook, " 'Immovables' and the 'Law' of the 'Situs,' " 52 *Harv. L. Rev.* 1246 (1939).

Ehrenzweig, "Contracts in Conflict of Laws," 59 *Colum. L. Rev.* 973, 1171 (1959).

Ehrenzweig, "The Lex Fori—Basic Rule in the Conflict of Laws," 58 *Mich. L. Rev.* 637 (1960).

Ehrenzweig, "The Statute of Frauds in the Conflict of Laws," 59 *Colum. L. Rev.* 874 (1959).

Ehrenzweig, "Torts, Contracts, Property, Status, Characterization and the Conflict of Laws," 59 *Colum. L. Rev.* 440 (1959).

Gorfinkel, "Conflict of Laws—A Survey of Past and Contemporary Theory," 16 *Hastings L. J.* 21 (1964).

Griswold, "Renvoi Revisited," 51 *Harv. L. Rev.* 1165 (1938).

Lorenzen, "Developments in Conflict of Laws, 1902–1942," 40 *Mich. L. Rev.* 781 (1942).

Misc., "Comments on *Babcock* v. *Jackson*, A Recent Development in Conflict of Laws," 63 *Colum. L. Rev.* 1212 (1963).

Reese, "Does Domicile Bear a Single Meaning?" 55 *Colum. L. Rev.* 589 (1955).

Reese and Flesch, "Agency and Vicarious Liability in Conflict of Laws," 60 *Colum. L. Rev.* 764 (1960).

Scoles, "Apportionment of Federal Estate Taxes and Conflict of Laws," 55 *Colum. L. Rev.* 261 (1955).

Shulman and Prevezer, "Torts in English and American Conflict of Laws: The Role of the Forum," 56 *Mich. L. Rev.* 1067 (1958).

Stern, "Foreign Law in the Courts," 45 *Calif. L. Rev.* 23 (1957).

CONSTITUTIONAL LAW

Avins, "The Fifteenth Amendment and Literacy Tests: The Original Intent," 18 *Stan L. Rev.* 808 (1966).

Berney, "Libel and the First Amendment—A New Constitutional Privilege," 51 *Va. L. Rev.* 1 (1965).

Fairman, "Does the Fourteenth Amendment Incorporate the Bill of Rights?" 2 *Stan L. Rev.* 5 (1949).

Frank and Munro, "The Original Understanding of 'Equal Protection of the Laws,' " 50 *Colum. L. Rev.* 131 (1950).

Granucci, " 'No Cruel and Unusual Punishments Inflicted': The Original Meaning," 57 *Calif. L. Rev.* 839 (1969).

Henderson, "The Background of the Seventh Amendment," 80 *Harv. L. Rev.* 289 (1966).

Howe, "The Meaning of 'Due Process of Law' Prior to the Adoption of the Fourteenth Amendment," 18 *Calif. L. Rev.* 583 (1930).

Johnston, "Sex Discrimination and the Supreme Court," 49 *N.Y.U. L. Rev.* 617 (1974).

Lewis, "The Meaning of 'State Action'," 60 *Colum. L. Rev.* 1083 (1960).

Mendelson, "Mr. Justice Frankfurter on the Construction of Statutes," 43 *Calif. L. Rev.* 652 (1955).

Mosk, "The Eighth Amendment Rediscovered," 1 *Loy. L. Rev.* 4 (1968).

Oaks, "Legal History in the High Court—Habeas Corpus," 64 *Mich. L. Rev.* 451 (1966).

Ratner, "The Function of the Due Process Clause," 116 *U. Pa. L. Rev.* 1048 (1968).

Rogge, "Unenumerated Rights (The Ninth Amendment)," 47 *Calif. L. Rev.* 787 (1959).

Ruud, "One-subject Rule," 42 *Minn. L. Rev.* 389 (1958).

ten Broeck, "Admissibility and Use by the United States Supreme Court of Extrinsic Aids in Constitutional Construction," 26 *Calif. L. Rev.* 287, 437, 664 (1938); 157, 399 (1939).

Van Alstyne and Karst, "State Action," 14 *Stan. L. Rev.* 3 (1961).

Wilkinson, "The Supreme Court, the Equal Protection Clause, and the Three Faces of Constitutionality," 61 *Va. L. Rev.* 945 (1975).

Wolfram, "Constitutional History of the Seventh Amendment," 57 *Minn. L. Rev.* 639 (1973).

"The Right to Counsel: A Symposium," 45 *Minn. L. Rev.* 693-896 (1961).

CONTRACTS

Blake, "Employee Agreements Not to Compete," 73 *Harv. L. Rev.* 625 (1960).

Boyer, "Promissory Estoppel," 50 *Mich. L. Rev.* 639, 873 (1952).

Childres, "Conditions in the Law of Contracts," 45 *N.Y.U. L. Rev.* 33 (1970).

Childres and Spitz, "Status in the Law of Contract," 47 *N.Y.U. L. Rev.* 1 (1972).

Corbin, "Recent Developments in the Law of Contracts," 50 *Harv. L. Rev.* 449 (1937).

Dawson, "Economic Duress—An Essay in Perspective," 45 *Mich. L. Rev.* 251 (1947).

Farnsworth, "Disputes Over Omission in Contracts," 68 *Colum. L. Rev.* 860 (1968).

Farnsworth, "Implied Warranties of Quality in Non-sales Cases," 57 *Colum. L. Rev.* 653 (1957).

Farnsworth, " 'Meaning' in the Law of Contracts," 76 *Yale L. J.* 939 (1967).

Farnsworth, "The Past of Promise: An Historical Introduction to Contract," 69 *Colum. L. Rev.* 576 (1969).

Ferson, "Contracts in Favor of Third Parties," 6 *Hastings L. J.* 354 (1955).

Henderson, "Promissory Estoppel and Traditional Contract Doctrine," 78 *Yale L. J.* 343 (1969).

Horwitz, "The Historical Foundations of Modern Contract Law," 87 *Harv. L. Rev.* 917 (1974).

Kepner, "Part Performance in Relation to Parol Contracts for the Sale of Lands," 35 *Minn. L. Rev.* 1 (1950).

McCall, "Repossession and Adhesion Contract Issues," 26 *Hastings L. J.* 383 (1974).

McGovern, "The Enforcement of Oral Covenants Prior to Assumpsit," 65 *Nw. U. L. Rev.* 576 (1970).

Palmer, "Reformation and the Parol Evidence Rule," 65 *Mich. L. Rev.* 833 (1967).

Paterson, "Freak-Tent of Contracts," 1 *Hastings L. J.* 141 (1950).

Patterson, "An Apology for Consideration," 58 *Colum. L. Rev.* 929 (1958).

Patterson, "The Interpretation and Construction of Contracts," 64 *Colum. L. Rev.* 833 (1964).

Rosett, "Contract Performance: Promises, Conditions and the Obligation to Communicate," 22 *U.C.L.A. L. Rev.* 1083 (1975).

Trimble, "The Law Merchant and the Letter of Credit," 61 *Harv. L. Rev.* 981 (1948).

CORPORATIONS

Berger, " 'Disregarding the Corporate Entity' for Stockholders' Benefit," 55 *Colum. L. Rev.* 808 (1955).

Conrad, "An Overview of the Laws of Corporations," 71 *Mich. L. Rev.* 621 (1973).

Mazumdar, "The Modern Corporation and the Rule of Law," 114 *U.Pa. L. Rev.* 187 (1965).

CRIMES

Blume, "The Place of Trial of Criminal Cases," 43 *Mich. L. Rev.* 59 (1944).

Calkins, "Grand Jury Secrecy," 63 *Mich. L. Rev.* 455 (1965).

Fletcher, "The Metamorphosis of Larceny," 89 *Harv. L. Rev.* 469 (1976).

Herman, "Warrants for Arrest or Search: Impeaching the Allegations of a Facially Sufficient Affidavit," 36 *Ohio St. L. J.* 721 (1975).

Oberer, "The Deadly Weapon Doctrine: Common Law Origin," 75 *Harv. L. Rev.* 1532 (1962).

Perkins, "The Act of One Conspirator," 26 *Hastings L. J.* 337 (1974).

Perkins, "An Analysis of Assault and Attempts to Assault," 47 *Minn. L. Rev.* 71 (1962).

Perkins, "A Rationale of Mens Rea," 52 *Harv. L. Rev.* 905 (1939).

Perkins, "The Territorial Principle in Criminal Law," 22 *Hastings L. J.* 1155 (1971).

Silten and Tullis, "Mental Competency in Criminal Proceedings," 28 *Hastings L. J.* 1053 (1977).

Smith, "Two Problems in Criminal Attempts," 70 *Harv. L. Rev.* 422 (1957).

EQUITY

Chafee, "Coming into Equity with Clean Hands," 47 *Mich. L. Rev.* 877, 1065 (1949).

Chesnin and Hazard, "Chancery Procedure and the Seventh Amendment: Jury Trial of Issues in Equity Cases before 1791," 83 *Yale L. J.* 999 (1974).

Newman, "The Hidden Equity," 19 *Hastings L. J.* 147 (1967).

Newman, "What Light is Cast by History on the Nature of Equity in Modern Law?" 17 *Hastings L. J.* 677 (1966).

Simpson, "Fifty Years of American Equity," 50 *Harv. L. Rev.* 171 (1936).

ETHICS

Curtis, "Ethics in the Law," 4 *Stan. L. Rev.* 477 (1952).

Curtis, "The Ethics of Advocacy," 4 *Stan. L. Rev.* 3 (1952).

EVIDENCE

Goodhart, "A Changing Approach to the Law of Evidence," 51 *Va. L. Rev.* 759 (1965).

FUTURE INTERESTS

Dukeminier, "Contingent Remainders and Executory Interests," 43 *Minn. L. Rev.* 13 (1958).

Leach, "Perpetuities in Perspective: Ending the Rule's Reign of Terror," 65 *Harv. L. Rev.* 721 (1951).

Leach, "Perpetuities: The Nutshell Revisited," 78 *Harv. L. Rev.* 973 (1965).

Leach and Logan, "Perpetuities: A Standard Savings Clause to Avoid Violations of the Rule," 74 *Harv. L. Rev.* 1141 (1961).

Powell, "The Rule Against Perpetuities and Spendthrift Trusts in New York," 71 *Colum. L. Rev.* 688 (1971).

LANDLORD AND TENANT

Love, "Landlord's Liability for Defective Premises," 1975 *Wis. L. Rev.* 19 (1975).

LEGAL HISTORY

Braybrooke, "Custom as a Source of English Law," 50 *Mich. L. Rev.* 71 (1951).

Green, "The Jury and the English Law of Homicide," 74 *Mich. L. Rev.* 413 (1976).

Noonan, "The Steady Man: Process and Policy in the Courts of the Roman Curia," 58 *Calif. L. Rev.* 628 (1970).

Pound, "The Role of the Will in Law," 68 *Harv. L. Rev.* 1 (1954).

Smith, "Administrative Control of the Courts of the American Plantations," 61 *Colum. L. Rev.* 121 (1961).

MOOT COURT

Honigman, "The Art of Appellate Advocacy," 64 *Mich. L. Rev.* 1055 (1966).

Marer, "Effective Criminal Appellate Advocacy," 27 *Hastings L. J.* 333 (1975).

Smith, "A Primer of Opinion Writing for Law Clerks," 26 *Vand. L. Rev.* 1203 (1973).

PLEADING AND PRACTICE

Semmel, "Collateral Estoppel, Mutuality and Joinder of Parties," 68 *Colum. L. Rev.* 1457 (1968).

PROPERTY

Browder, "Rule Against Perpetuities," 62 *Mich. L. Rev.* 1 (1963).

Hogan, "The Innkeepers Lien at Common Law," 8 *Hastings L. J.* 33 (1956).

Lund, "Early American Wildlife Law," 51 *N.Y.U. L. Rev.* 703 (1976).

McGovern, "The Historical Conception of a Lease for Years," 23 *U.C.L.A. L. Rev.* 501 (1976).

Newman and Losey, "Covenants Running with the Land and Equitable Servitude," 21 *Hastings L. J.* 1319 (1970).

Paulus, "*Finder* v. *Locus*, in Quo—An Outline," 6 *Hastings L. J.* 180 (1955).

Rabin, "The Law Favors the Vesting of Estates. Why?" 65 *Colum. L. Rev.* 467 (1965).

QUASI-CONTRACTS

Perillo, "Restitution in a Contractual Context," 73 *Colum. L. Rev.* 1208 (1973).

RESTITUTION

Thurston, "Recent Developments in Restitution 1940–1947," 45 *Mich. L. Rev.* 935 (1947).

Thurston, "Recent Developments in Restitution: Recission and Reformation for Mistake, Including Misrepresentation," 46 *Mich. L. Rev.* 1037 (1948).

TAXATION

Browder, "Trusts and the Doctrine of Estates," 72 *Mich. L. Rev.* 1507 (1974).

TORTS

Calabresi, "Concerning Cause and the Law of Torts," 43 *U. Chi. L. Rev.* 69 (1975).

Calabresi and Hirschoff, "Toward a Test for Strict Liability in Torts," 81 *Yale L. J.* 1055 (1972).

Gordon, "The Unborn Plaintiff," 63 *Mich. L. Rev.* 579 (1965).

Green, "The Causal Relation Issue in Negligence Law," 60 *Mich. L. Rev.* 543 (1962).

James and Thornton, "Impact of Insurance on the Law of Torts," 15 *Law and Contemp. Prob.* 431 (1950).

Keeton, "Conditional Fault in the Law of Torts," 72 *Harv. L. Rev.* 401 (1959).

Keeton, "Trespass, Nuisance and Strict Liability," 59 *Colum. L. Rev.* 457 (1959).

Prosser, "Comparative Negligence," 51 *Mich. L. Rev.* 465 (1953).

Prosser, "False Imprisonment: Consciousness of Confinement," 55 *Colum. L. Rev.* 847 (1955).

Prosser, "Injurious Falsehood: The Basis of Liability," 59 *Colum. L. Rev.* 425 (1959).

Prosser, "Insult and Outrage," 44 *Calif. L. Rev.* 40 (1956).

Prosser, "Palsgraf Revisited," 52 *Mich. L. Rev.* 1 (1953).

Prosser, "Privacy," 48 *Calif. L. Rev.* 383 (1960).

Seavey, "Nuisance: Contributory Negligence and Other Mysteries," 65 *Harv. L. Rev.* 984 (1951).

Stone, "Touchstones of Tort Liability," 2 *Stan. L. Rev.* 259 (1950).

TRUSTS

Scott, "The Fiduciary Principle," 37 *Calif. L. Rev.* 539 (1949).

Scott, "Restitution from an Innocent Transferee Who Is Not a Purchaser for Value," 62 *Harv. L. Rev.* 1022 (1948).

WILLS

Halbach, "Stare Decisis and Rules of Construction in Wills and Trusts," 52 *Calif. L. Rev.* 921 (1964).

McGovern, "Homicide and Succession to Property," 68 *Mich. L. Rev.* 65 (1969).

Pound, "The Role of the Will in Law," 68 *Harv. L. Rev.* 1 (1954).

Sparks, "Enforcement of Contracts to Devise or Bequeath After the Death of the Promisor," 39 *Minn. L. Rev.* 1 (1954).

MISCELLANEOUS

Cahn, "Authority and Responsibility," 51 *Colum. L. Rev.* 839 (1951).

Cappelletti and Gordley, "Legal Aid: Modern Theories and Variations," 24 *Stan. L. Rev.* 347 (1972).

Christie, "Vagueness and Legal Language," 48 *Minn. L. Rev.* 885 (1964).

Cohen, "Thomas Jefferson Recommends a Course of Law Study," 119 *U. Pa. L. Rev.* 823 (1971).

Finkelstein and Fairley, "A Comment on Trial by Mathematics," 84 *Harv. L. Rev.* 1801 (1971).

Hancock, " 'In the Parish of St. Mary Le Bow, in the Ward of Cheap,' " 16 *Stan. L. Rev.* 516 (1964).

Hills, "The Law of Accounting," 54 *Colum. L. Rev.* 1, 1049 (1954).

Kenyon, "Legal Lore of the Wild West. A Bibliographical Essay," 56 *Calif. L. Rev.* 681 (1968).

Nagel and Weitzman, "Women as Litigants," 23 *Hastings L. J.* 171 (1971).

Newman, "Similarity of Doctrines in Legal Systems," 18 *Hastings L. J.* 481 (1967).

Shapiro, "Law and Science in Seventeenth-Century England," 21 *Stan. L. Rev.* 722 (1969).

Silving, "The Unknown and Unknowable in Law," 35 *Calif. L. Rev.* 352 (1947).

Stein, "The Attraction of the Civil Law in Post-Revolutionary America," 52 *Va. L. Rev.* 403 (1966).

Stevens, "Law Schools and Law Students," 59 *Va. L. Rev.* 551 (1973).

Stone, "Legal Education on the Couch," 85 *Harv. L. Rev.* 392 (1971).

Touster, "Holmes: The Years of the Common Law," 64 *Colum. L. Rev.* 230 (1964).

Tribe, "Further Critique of Mathematical Proof," 84 *Harv. L. Rev.* 1810 (1971).

Tribe, "Trial by Mathematics: Precision and Ritual in the Legal Process," 84 *Harv. L. Rev.* 1329 (1971).

Trubek, "Toward a Social Theory of Law: An Essay on the Study of Law and Development," 82 *Yale L. J.* 1 (1972).

White, "The Rise and Fall of Justice Holmes," 39 *U. Chi. L. Rev.* 51 (1971).

Williams, "The Concept of Legal Liberty," 56 *Colum. L. Rev.* 1129 (1956).

"The Common Law Origins of the Infield Fly Rule," 123 *U. Pa. L. Rev.* 1474 (1975).

"Uniformity in Financial Accounting," 30 *Law and Contemp. Prob.* 621–931 (1965).

GLOSSSARY OF LEGAL TERMS

Here are some of the words and phrases you will run into at law school. They are defined in nonlegal language to make it easier for you to do your preliminary orientation reading. When you actually get into your casebooks, be sure to look up the precise definitions in your law dictionary.

abandon: give up all claims or rights to something.
abate: put an end to some situation.
abet: urge someone to commit a criminal act.
ab initio: going back to the beginning.
absentee: individual who is not present.
abstract: short version of a case or of a public record.
abut: to be adjacent to.
accept: knowingly receive or agree.
acceptance: response to an offer in anticipation of entering into a contract.
accession: increase in real or personal property.
accessory: party to a criminal act.
accessory after the fact: person aiding a criminal after the commission of the crime.

accessory before the fact: person participating in the planning of a crime, but absent at its actual commission.

accident: an injury for which there is no legal remedy.

accomplice: party to a criminal act.

accord and satisfaction: settlement of a claim for less than the full amount.

account stated: an agreement between debtor and creditor as to the balance due.

accretion: gradual increase in the size of land adjacent to water because of silt, rock, or sand accumulation.

accrue: reach a certain point in time or growth.

accusation: initial administrative law charging document.

acknowledgment: declaration before a notary public that the maker has signed a document.

acquittal: finding of not guilty in a criminal case.

action: a suit in the law or equity courts.

actionable negligence: conduct which gives rise to an action in tort for damages.

action at law: a case coming before the law courts.

action in equity: a case coming before the equity courts.

action on the case: action at common law for damages where no willful force was used.

act of God: event which occurs without human intervention.

act of law: governmental intervention which interferes with intentions of parties dealing with each other.

adeem: to diminish a legacy because of gifts prior to death.

adjective law: laws and rules relating to pleading, practice, and evidence.

administrative agency: a governmental agency which makes and enforces rules and regulations in a specialized field.

administrative law: branch of law dealing with regulations by, and hearings before, administrative agencies.

advance sheets: interim paperback supplements to volumes of reported cases, containing new cases, which later are incorporated in a new volume when the quantity is sufficient.

adverse possession: holding of real property without legal right.

affirmance: appellate court ruling that the lower court correctly tried the case.

affirmative duty: special duty required by law in conduct toward others.

aiding and abetting: being present and helping commit a crime without actually taking part in the criminal act itself.

allegation: statement of fact in a pleading.

annotation: citations following a statute showing the cases where the statute has been mentioned.

answer: written document responding to the allegations of a complaint.

appellant: party appealing decision of lower court.

appellate court: court to which appeal may be taken having power to overrule or reverse decision of trial or lower court.

asportation: taking of goods illegally.

assault: attempt to commit a battery which falls short of actually touching the intended victim.

assumpsit: action on a contract at common law.

assumption of risk: putting oneself in a position where injury might normally be expected to occur.

at issue: case is ready for trial.

attempt: an act intended to culminate in a crime, but which is never finalized by commission of the crime.

bail: a sum of money or other security deposited in court to guarantee a person's appearance for trial.

battery: trespass to the person where there is an actual touching.

beneficiary: individual benefiting from a trust, or from a contract made by other parties.

bequest: gift of personal property made in a will.

bilateral contract: contract in which both parties are bound to do something.

Blackacre: used to describe a hypothetical parcel of land in real property class discussions.

bona fide: good faith.

brief: a written legal argument submitted to an appellate court.

burden of proof: the duty on the part of a litigant to convince the trier of fact that his or her side of the case should prevail.

burglary: at common law, breaking into a dwelling at night.

calendared: set on court's docket for hearing at a specified time.

case: a lawsuit generally; also, a particular action at common law to recover money damages.

casebook: law school book containing reported appellate cases on a particular subject arranged to present an orderly development of that area of law.

case in point: a case pertaining to the rule of law under discussion.

case law: the law found in the decisions of the appellate courts.

case method: law school teaching method using opinions of appellate courts for source material.

cause: a lawsuit.

cause of action: basic elements which must be proved in order to have a valid lawsuit.

caveat emptor: let the buyer beware.

chancery: the courts of equity.

citation: volume, page, and reporter where a case may be found.

class action: law suit on behalf of number of persons not specifically named.

code: group of statutes, usually consolidated by subject.

common law: law developed by judges through written opinions.

common law pleading: the entire system of presenting the facts and issues of a case to a court through documents filed before the trial starts.

comparative negligence: a doctrine in the law of torts where the jury assesses the damages based upon its finding as to what percentage of fault it allocates to each party.

complainant: the person instituting a suit in an action at law.

complaint: initial document filed in a lawsuit.

compounding a felony: victim agreeing not to prosecute in exchange for being repaid or bribed not to testify.

confession and avoidance: a common law pleading admitting the facts alleged but adding something new to alter the interpretation of those facts.

conflict of laws: a branch of the law dealing with the law to be applied by the court when the events of the case occurred in two states.

consideration: the ultimate basis of a contract; some act or promise given in exchange for another act or promise.

conspiracy: agreement between two or more persons to commit some illegal act.

contract: a legally enforceable agreement.

contributory negligence: an act by the plaintiff which contributed to the injury.

conveyance: a deed.

close: the land and buildings around a dwelling house.

county court: local trial court.

court below: trial court or lower appellate court.

crime: violation of some law which is punishable by some governmental entity.

cross offers: offers relating to the same subject matter sent by opposing parties to each other simultaneously.

damages: amount of money awarded to the victorious plaintiff in a lawsuit.

decedent: a dead person.

decedent's estate: a dead person's assets subject to the jurisdiction of a probate court.

decision: the court determination as to which side won the lawsuit.

declaration: original charging document filed in lawsuit at common law; a statement under oath in writing.

defendant: the person sued in an action at law.

demurrer: a pleading which in effect admits the facts alleged in the complaint but argues that even if they are true, the complaint fails to state a cause of action.

digest: set of index books containing the headnotes of a particular series of reports arranged by legal topic.

dilatory plea: a plea at common law which could stop the case from proceeding until the point raised was cleared up.

district court: the lowest court in the federal trial system.

domicile: a person's permanent home.

easement: right to use another's land in a certain manner.

elements of a cause of action: those things which must be alleged and proved in order to show that the plaintiff has a valid cause of action.

entrapment: tricking someone into committing a crime.

equity: that branch of law dealing with the court's right to give remedies other than money damages.

estate: a right in real property; an individual's assets.

exception: in the older cases, the trial lawyer had to object, and then take exception to a judge's ruling, if he wished to preserve the right to contest the ruling on appeal.

execution of judgment: enforcement of the ruling of a court.

exhaustion of administrative remedies: legal doctrine that prevents a person from suing in a court on a matter within the province of an administrative agency until all remedies permitted by the agency are first taken.

false imprisonment: confining someone's ability to move about freely without any legal right to keep the person restricted.

federal court: a court in the federal judicial system.

fee: title to land.

fee simple: full title to land.

felony: a serious crime punishable by imprisonment or death.

feudal system: the ancient English method of land ownership and allegiance to the king through a pyramidal system running through serfs, through their knights, through various higher nobles, up to the ruler.

first degree murder: killing with intent, premeditation and deliberation.

fixtures: personal property items attached to realty.

forseeable: a reasonable man could anticipate the consequences.

future interests: a branch of the law of real property dealing with the rights of persons coming after the grantor and grantee.

general damages: estimated damages set by the jury, over and above actual out-of-pocket expenses, arising as a result of the defendant's conduct.

general issue: defendant's plea asking for jury trial at common law.

general intent: criminal law concept which allows certain crimes to be proven even though no specific intent is shown.

gift: something of value transferred to another without consideration.

grand jury: group of people chosen in a county by the court who hand down indictments for crimes.